JERUSALEM
and the Holy Land

By the staff of Editions Berlitz

Berlitz Trademark Reg. U.S. Patent Office and other countries –
Marca Registrada.

Library of Congress Catalog Card No. 79-84592.

Printed in Switzerland by Weber SA, Bienne.

Updated edition 1981

Preface

A new kind of travel guide for the jet age—and one of an extensive series by Berlitz on the world's top tourist areas—this compact and colourful book is packed with all you need to know about Jerusalem and the Holy Land.

Like our phrase books and dictionaries, this book fits your pocket—in both size and price. It also aims to fit your travel needs:

- It combines easy reading with fast facts: what to see and do, where to shop, what to eat.

- An authoritative A-to-Z "blueprint" fills the back of the book, giving clear-cut answers to all your questions, from "Where can I change traveller's cheques after normal banking hours?" to "Is the water safe to drink?" plus special sections on planning your budget, how to get there and when to go.

- Easy-to-read maps in full colour pinpoint sights you'll want to see.

In short, this handy guide will enhance your enjoyment of Israel. From the holy sites of the Old City of Jerusalem to the brash modern metropolis of Tel Aviv, from Tiberias and the Mount of Beatitudes to Qumran and the Dead Sea Scrolls—Berlitz tells you clearly and concisely what it's all about.

How to use this guide
If time is short, look for items to visit which are printed in bold type in this book, e.g. **Citadel of David.** Those sights most highly recommended are not only given in bold type but also carry our traveller symbol, e.g. **Church of the Holy Sepulchre.**

Area specialist: Tom Brosnahan
Photography: Erling Mandelmann
We are particularly grateful to Ronald Miller for his help in the preparation of this book. We also wish to thank the Israel Government Tourist Office and El Al Israel Airlines for their valuable assistance.
Cartography: Falk-Verlag, Hamburg.

Contents

Maps: Jerusalem—Old City p. 23, Central Jerusalem pp. 54–55, Excursions p. 73, Tel Aviv–Jaffa p. 81.
Cover: View over Jerusalem and the Dome of the Rock from the Russian Orthodox Church of Mary Magdalene (foreground).

The City and the People

No matter how extravagant your expectations, Jerusalem can fulfil them. Holy City to Jews, Christians and Moslems, capital of modern Israel, dynamic metropolis, Jerusalem succeeds in being most things to most people.

Above all, it is a city for visitors, and in a very real sense a second home to every Jew, Christian and Moslem in the world. Though it may take a while to get accustomed to the Old City's lacework of lanes and alleys and to sort out the Judean hills and dales, from your first moment in Jerusalem you will feel that you know the place in spirit and that you belong.

Jerusalemites of every faith are eager to make visitors welcome, whatever the reason for their trip. You can watch a group of black-bearded Ortho-

dox Jews shepherding sons and grandsons to the venerable Western Wall for prayer, or stop and enjoy the sonorous chanting of the muezzins who call the faithful to noontime devotions from the minaret of El-Aksa Mosque; or go along with the Franciscan monks, who will explain the significance of the fourteen Stations of the Cross along the Via Dolorosa. After a tiring day's pilgrimage and sightseeing, you can relax in Jerusalem's comfortable hotels, hospices and restaurants.

Despite the friendly welcome, the city lives its history every day. Mutual respect is usually the rule among the many denominations and sects of the three great religions, but this is sacred ground and has had more blood spilled on it for

Reverence for tradition and zest for life; a bar mitzvah at the Western Wall, and a comely smile.

its own sake than any other place in the world. Rivalries lie dormant and do not disappear. Don't be surprised to find a soldier, submachine gun slung across his shoulder, seated watchfully in a bus, a café or a park; it is this kind of vigilance that keeps the city peaceful.

Being at the centre of the religious world brings a bewildering diversity to life in Jerusalem. A dozen languages echo from the dome above the Church of the Holy Sepulchre, and some of the shopkeepers in the labyrinthine bazaars speak all of them and more. Nowhere else on earth are you likely to see such a variety of costumes. Hassidic Jews wear black hats and tail-coats, a traditional garb dating from the origin of their sect in 18th-century eastern Europe. Arabs are clad in flowing robes and *keffiyes* (head scarves), or jackets and fezzes, or blue jeans and T-shirts. Nuns in their habits, tourists in Bermuda shorts, Israeli women in military uniforms, berobed Orthodox priests and Bedouin women in richly embroidered dresses all vie for seats on buses, wait at traffic lights and haggle over vegetables in the bazaars. These colourful contrasts are further enriched by the customs and cuisines of the thousands of Jews who have moved to the Promised Land since the founding of modern Israel in 1948.

Since that year hundreds of thousands of immigrants, displaced persons, refugees and survivors of the Nazi holocaust have been offered sanctuary in the new state. Despite difficult political and economic conditions for everyone, determination plus the application of modern techniques to the economy has given the majority a roof over their heads and enough to eat.

The population of Israel is about 3½ million, of whom some 2,960,000 are Jews, 410,000 Moslems and 80,000 Christians. There are also about 46,000 Druze—members of a religious sect which broke away from Islam in the 11th century—most of whom live in villages in the Galilee region.

The Jewish people are formed by two main groups, the Ashkenazim and the Sephardim. The Ashkenazim come from central Europe, whereas the Sephardim are descended from Jews exiled from Spain in 1492 at the time of the

To whom does Jerusalem belong? In spirit, it's everyone's. **9**

Inquisition. More than half a dozen other groups add their own traditions to the community. The mystical Hassidim from Poland, dark-skinned Cochin Jews from India, Jews from Iraq, from Tunisia, Morocco, the Yemen and many other countries all come together in Israel. Their children, the sabras, constitute nearly 45 per cent of the Jewish population.

But, wherever they come from, and however different their customs may be on points of detail, the Jewish people are united by their faith in the Torah (the first five books of the Bible) and the Talmud (a collection of commentaries, laws and oral traditions handed down from generation to generation from its conception in the 5th century A.D.).

You'll sense some of this unity as you plunge into the sights, sounds and colours of this fascinating city. But you'll also find that planning your day is no easy matter. Each religion has a different Sabbath and a different calendar of religious holidays. A day's itinerary is often confounded as shops, offices, mosques and museums are opened or shut for religious or patriotic festivals, prayers, traditions, or just a summer afternoon's siesta.

But if some places close abruptly, others open just as suddenly—Jerusalem is never completely at rest.

In the midst of the confusion is a passion for continuity. Any change must take into account the sensitivies of a hundred beliefs and traditions: even as little as moving a candlestick

Hebrew University's modern structures echo those of ancient times. Walls of tawny Jerusalem limestone have the look of petrified sunlight.

may bring up objections. By general agreement and city ordinance, all buildings must be faced with tawny limestone, keeping the city Jerusalem the Golden. Perhaps this kind of mutual respect and cooperation will be the Holy City's salvation after so many centuries of strife.

11

A Brief History

The Bible is our best source for the history of early Jerusalem. In Bronze Age times, around 1850 B.C., "Urusalim" or "Salem" was ruled by a king called Melchizedek. Genesis tells us that he once blessed Abraham, giving him bread and wine *(Gen. 14:18–20)*. Later, when God made his covenant with Abraham, part of it called for his descendants to conquer many lands. One of them was Canaan, in which lay the city of Urusalim.

In the centuries between 1400 and 1000 B.C., the tribes of Israel conquered all the lands north and south of Jerusalem, leaving the fortified city as the only undefeated spot in the territory. Then, around 1000 B.C., the chiefs of the tribes of Israel elected David, a young man of some 30 years from Bethlehem, to be their king.

The Kingdoms of David and Solomon

Not wanting to set a dangerous precedent by favouring one or another of the tribal towns for the establishment of his court, King David prepared to march on Jerusalem, then called Jebus. He intended to make it his royal city. Finding out about the Jebusites' secret water tunnel under the walls, the Israelites slipped into the city and took it by surprise *(2 Sam. 5:8)*.

The king strengthened the walls and the fortress called Zion. He brought in the Ark of the Covenant to make Jerusalem a Holy City. The might of the kingdom grew, and by the time his son Solomon succeeded him around 965 B.C., almost all of the extensive and potentially wealthy lands between the Nile and the Euphrates belonged to Israel.

King Solomon ruled during the Golden Age of Hebrew Jerusalem. The king is remembered not only for his proverbial wisdom, but also for the construction of the First Temple, on land which his father had purchased from the defeated king of the Jebusites. The plot of land was north of the small Davidic city, on top of Mount Moriah (now the site of the Dome of the Rock). Used in earlier times as a threshing-place, it was, legend says, the spot where Abraham's near-sacrifice of Isaac had been made. The First Temple was impressive more for its beauty and elegance than for its size. Along with the splendid house of worship, Solomon built a royal palace, mansions for his wives, barracks for his guards, and towers for the defence of the capital.

But the Golden Age lasted barely a century, from David's conquest to the death of King Solomon. Later monarchs were never able to reign in such power and glory as he had. In 701 B.C. the Assyrian armies of Sennacherib besieged Jerusalem, and it narrowly escaped destruction. The end of David's dynasty came in 587 B.C. when Nebuchadnezzar, King of Babylon, invaded Judah to lay siege to Jerusalem *(2 Kings 24,25)*. When it fell, the Temple and all the buildings were put to the torch. The people of the once-glorious city were forced into exile.

In time the kingdom of Babylon was overthrown, and the Israelites began to return to Jerusalem. The city was now (539 B.C.) under the more tolerant rule of the Persians. Rebuilding was slow work. The Second Temple was finished in 515 B.C., but much of the city still lay in ruins.

Jerusalem gave in peaceably to the world-rule of Alexander the Great (332 B.C.), and in following centuries to that of the Egyptians and Seleucids as well. Then, in the 2nd century, Jews led by Judas Maccabeus revolted against the Seleucids and restored the primacy of Jewish religious life in Jerusalem. The reconsecration of the Temple, accomplished in 164 B.C., has been commemorated ever since in the ceremonies of Hanukkah (Feast of Dedication). The Maccabeans formed the Hasmonean dynasty and ruled until the coming of Pompey's Roman legions, in 63 B.C.

Romans and Christians

After the initial few years of Roman administration and political infighting, Herod the Great was made King of Judea. He reigned from 40 to 4 B.C. during which time he built up the city. He constructed a fortress with three massive towers, parts of which still stand today. Several palaces were erected and a modern water system installed. Temple Mount was shored up by walls made with great stone blocks. (One of these walls, the Western Wall, was later to become a symbol of Jewish longings for Jerusalem's vanished greatness.) Herod also rebuilt the Temple itself, and put up a strong fortress nearby. He named it Antonia, in honour of his Roman friend and benefactor Mark Antony.

In addition to all the construction work, Herod did everything he could to beautify **13**

Jesus shares Passover seder in Giotto's Last Supper *(Padua).*

the city and glorify himself but he never succeeded in getting his subjects to love him. It wasn't surprising, as this was the same Herod the Great, rebuilder of Jerusalem, who ordered the massacre of all newborn babies in an attempt to do away with the heralded Messiah *(Matt. 2:16)*. Joseph and Mary escaped the wrath and paranoia of Herod by fleeing into Egypt with the infant Jesus.

Jesus was born in Bethlehem, Joseph's ancestral home, in about 6 B.C.* After returning from Egypt, his parents lived in Nazareth, but they used to come up to Jerusalem every year for Passover. When Jesus was about thirty years old, he went to be baptized by John, an ascetic preacher living in the wilds of the Jordan valley *(Matt. 3:13–16)*.

Not long afterwards he embarked on a period of travelling and teaching which lasted for about three years. Much of the time was spent in Galilee, a

André Held, Ecublens

─────────────
* The exact year of Jesus' birth is uncertain; most sources give the date as around 6 B.C.

15

province north of Judea, but his influence was so great among the people that even the Temple priests and government officers in Jerusalem knew about his work. Jesus' lessons were simple and matter-of-fact, but they put in question much religious and legal tradition, and were therefore a threat to the priests and secular rulers.

After his years of teaching, Jesus and his followers went to Jerusalem for Passover. The Holy City at this time was a powder-keg of dissatisfaction with Roman domination and the rule of Herod Antipas, son of Herod the Great. Jesus' triumphal entry into the city caused a commotion and soon afterwards he was arrested by the Temple priests (Luke 22:54) who governed in Herod's name. He was tried quickly on Thursday evening and Friday morning by the Sanhedrin, or supreme rabbinical court. The Sanhedrin's members found him guilty of blasphemy and sentenced him to death (Matt. 26:63–66). But the sentence could only be carried out if confirmed by the Roman procurator, Pontius Pilate. Pilate was in a difficult situation: he could find no evidence against Jesus, but if he said 'no' to the powerful priests and didn't confirm the sentence he might have riots in the city. He tried to escape his responsibility by "washing his hands" of the affair (Matt. 27:24), but nevertheless handed over the prisoner in his charge. The sentence was carried out quickly on Friday, before sunset brought the beginning of the Passover Sabbath. On the third day after his death, according to Christian belief, he was resurrected.

Destruction of Jerusalem

After Jesus' crucifixion, the delicate balance of Jewish municipal government under Roman overlordship continued in Jerusalem until A.D. 66 when the city rebelled against the Romans. For four years the Jewish Zealots fought against the might of Rome. At the end, in A.D. 70, Titus the Roman general laid siege to the city, finally attacking its starved and weakened defenders. Those who didn't escape were executed or sold into slavery and the Holy City was totally destroyed. The last of the Zealots held out for another three years at Masada (see p. 75).

For some 60 years Jerusalem lay in ruins, until the Roman Emperor Hadrian rebuilt the town in the 2nd century, naming it Aelia Capitolina. Except for the Jewish revolt of Bar Kokhba (A.D. 132–135), the new town remained relatively peaceful and people lived from day to day with little excitement.

All this changed when the Roman Empire became Christian in the 4th century. Jerusalem suddenly acquired new and great significance. Empress Helena, a Christian and the mother of Constantine the Great, took a particular interest in the city and its holy places. A church was built around Golgotha (the hill where Jesus' crucifixion had taken place), and other spots important to Jesus' life were found and commemorated. Pilgrims came from throughout the Roman (and later, Byzantine) Empire during the centuries which followed, but the prosperity they brought lasted only until 614, when ferocious Persian armies overran Judea and reduced Jerusalem to rubble once more.

Still reeling from the effects of the Persian devastation Jerusalem was conquered soon afterwards (638) by the forces of Islam. The city was very important in Moslem eyes, as according to Islam, Mohammed had been summoned by angels while he slept in Mecca and rode a magic steed into the heavens, travelling as far as Jerusalem. The "farthest spot" (in Arabic El-Aksa) that he reached was the site of Temple Mount. To this day, the Dome of the Rock, built in 691, remains one of Jerusalem's most striking monuments.

Jerusalem was subject to Moslem rule for most of the years between the 7th and 11th centuries. Then, in 1099, under their leaders Tancred and Godfrey de Bouillon, the Crusaders captured the Holy City for Christendom.

Crusaders, Mamelukes and Turks

The Crusaders established a feudal state with Godfrey at its head. They built many impressive churches during the short term of the first Latin Kingdom of Jerusalem (1099–1187) but were later driven out by the Kurdish Moslem warrior Saladin. Then, in the Sixth Crusade (1228–29), Frederick II, the Holy Roman emperor, managed to secure Jerusalem for the Crusaders by negotiation.

But the Christians couldn't hold the city from the surrounding sea of Islam, and by the mid-13th century the Mamelukes of Egypt had taken complete control of the land, **17** ruling Jerusalem in relative peace for the next two and a half centuries. Much of the best architecture in the city dates from Mameluke times.

In the early 16th century, the Ottomans, a Turkish dynasty which had absorbed the remnants of the derelict Byzantine empire in the 14th and 15th centuries, were extending their power throughout the Middle East. Jerusalem fell to them in 1517 and remained under their control for the next 400 years. Suleiman the Magnificent, the powerful Ottoman sultan, took a special interest in Jerusalem, rebuilding the walls and gates in the form they retain to this day. Fountains, inns, religious colleges and barracks were constructed, and the city flourished as long as he was sultan. But when Suleiman died, the great empire began a long period of decline, and Jerusalem declined along with it. For 300 years the Holy City remained a backwater, until the 19th century, when renewed interest among Christian pilgrims made it the goal of thousands of travellers each year.

19th-Century Aspirations and the British Mandate

At this time another group of Europeans was also interested in the city and the region. Many

One man's dream inspired the Jewish return to Israel. His name is sufficient epitaph: Herzl.

Jews sought religious freedom and fulfilment by moving to Palestine, and especially to Jerusalem. In the last decades of the 19th century, Theodor Herzl (1860–1904) worked to organize the Zionist movement whose aim was the formation of a Jewish state. Chaim Weizmann (1874–1952), a scientist born in Russia but later a British subject, did much to put the theories of Herzl into practice. Weizmann was an important figure in the negotiations with the British which ended with the Balfour Declaration in 1917. The declaration supported the idea of a Jewish "national home" in Palestine, with full respect for the rights of the existing non-Jewish peoples already living there, but the problem was that British strategists, who had gained control from the Turks in 1917, had secretly promised the lands to their First World War Arab allies.

In 1922, the League of Nations granted the British a mandate to administer Palestine. It lasted until 1948 during which time Zionists battled

Arab nationalists for control of the territory. Each side had a weighty claim to the land based on history and religion, and each was supported by a part of the British administration. Power plays, legal wrangles and even gun battles broke the peace as both sides fought their opponents and the British overlords. In 1947, the United Nations voted for the partition of Palestine into two states, one Jewish, one Arab, with Jerusalem as an international city that belonged to neither. But lacking the means to enforce its decision, the United Nations was powerless to halt the bitter strife which broke out as the British withdrew their troops in 1948.

Modern Israel

The State of Israel was declared during this difficult time, with Chaim Weizmann as first president. In response, member states of the Arab League sent troops to help the Palestinian Arabs. Jerusalem and the whole region were carved up by battle lines.

Armistice agreements were reached early in 1949. Israel held the land granted by the U.N. decision and the Arab League states received most of the parts once destined to be a Palestinian Arab state. Jeru-

salem became a divided city, with the western portion in Israeli territory, the eastern portion including the Old City and the holy places in Jordanian territory.

In the 20 years that followed, Jerusalem was actually two cities. Both geographical and human divisions were aggravated by occasional incidents of terrorism or sniping across the partition lines, until the Six-Day War in June 1967. Within three days the city was

Centuries of conquest and construction made Jerusalem the world's grandest architectural museum: skyline testifies to turbulent history.

completely in Israeli hands, and two weeks later it was physically and administratively reunited.

For most people, reading the daily newspaper is to participate in the continuing saga of Jerusalem's battles and treaties, politics and passions. Cultural reunification has proved more difficult than removing barbed wire or breaking down stone walls. The prevailing mood in the city is usually something of a cool respect and resignation to the idea of living and working together. While all Jerusalemites yearn for peace, true brotherhood is for the future, in better days.

What to See

There are various organized tours which can be useful for general orientation at the beginning of your stay. Details will be obtainable from your hotel or any tourist office. But the best way to discover Jerusalem is on foot. For most pilgrims, the end of the journey comes only after they have penetrated the tawny walls of the Old City, which is where we'll start. (For opening hours refer to pages 120–122.)

💼 The Old City

The Old City is large by medieval standards, but quite small by modern ones. Its streets are narrow, full of twisting lanes, oriental *souks*, steep stairways and dark, covered passageways. It will take you several days before the maze becomes familiar, several more before the principal landmarks become easily identifiable.

A good place to set off on a visit to the Old City is the **Jaffa Gate,** a pair of massive medieval towers which form part of the Citadel of David, prime bastion of the city for thousands of years. Just through the gate is a branch of the Israel Government Tourist Office, and beside it two quaint old Moslem tombs behind an iron fence, shaded by fig trees and an ancient cypress.

The **Citadel of David** has two entrances, one to the right before you enter Jaffa Gate, and one a short distance along the road through the gate. The latter is the more interesting: built by Suleiman the Magnificent in 1531–32, it bears inscriptions in three varieties of Arabic script, and leads to a bridge over the remains of the Citadel's moat. Take some time here: mount the stairs to the roof and battlements for views of the city and explore the ruins and excavations. Jerusalem's municipal museum is set up in the Citadel, with displays outlining the history of the city. If you return in the evening, you can witness a dramatic sound-and-light show held under the stars in the courtyard (see p. 92).

Across the street from the moat entrance to the Citadel is Christ Church, the oldest Anglican church in the Middle East (1849). There are also a few cafés, as well as several convenient public services including a bank, post office, telephone kiosk and a police station.

The south-western part of the Old City, surrounding the

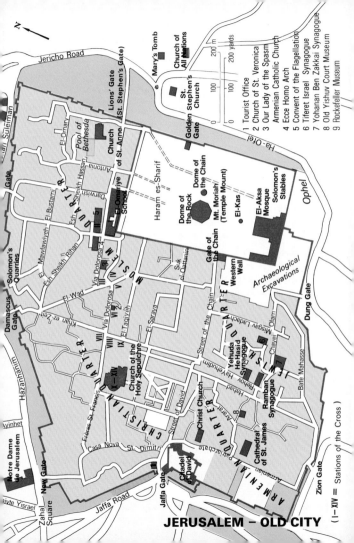

JERUSALEM – OLD CITY

(I – XIV = Stations of the Cross)

1 Tourist Office
2 Church of St. Veronica
3 Our Lady of the Spasm
  Armenian Catholic Church
4 Ecce Homo Arch
5 Convent of the Flagellation
6 Tiferet Israel Synagogue
7 Yohanan Ben Zakkai Synagogue
8 Old Yishuv Court Museum
9 Rockefeller Museum

Jericho Road

N

200 m
200 yards
100
100

Mary's Tomb
Church of All Nations
St. Stephen's Church
Lions' Gate (St. Stephen's Gate)
Golden Gate
Ha-Ofel

El-Omariye School
Pool of Bethesda
Church of St. Anne
Antonia
Darwish Hassan
Esh Sheikh Hassan
El-Bustami

Gate
Bab Suleiman
El-Omary
Esh Sheikh Rihan
El Mawazwiyen

MOSLEM QUARTER

Haram es-Sharif
Dome of the Rock
Dome of the Chain
Mt. Moriah (Temple Mount)
El-Kas
El-Aksa Mosque
Solomon's Stables

Ophel

Solomon's Quarries
Damascus Gate

Via Dolorosa III
Via Dolorosa
El Wad
Khan ez-Zeit
Via Dolorosa
El Taqiyeh
El Saraya
Suk el Dattania
Gate of the Chain

Western Wall
Archaeological Excavations

Dung Gate

JEWISH QUARTER
Street of the Chain
Misgav Ladach
Olam
Chayei

CHRISTIAN QUARTER
Church of the Holy Sepulchre
Frères St. François
Hazannanim
Notre Dame de Jérusalem
New Gate
Zahal Square
Zivyte Yisrael
Ayinhet

Casa Nova
St. Dimitri
Christ Church
Street of David
Habad
Hayehudim
Rehov HaYehudim
Yehuda HeHasid Synagogue
Rambam Synagogue
Bate Mahasse
Ararat
Aviram

Jaffa Road
Jaffa Gate
Citadel of David

ARMENIAN QUARTER
Cathedral of St. James
Armenian Patriarchate
Zion Gate

Citadel of David, is the **Armenian Quarter** and has been inhabited by this staunch Christian people since early times. Up the hill past the police station, a short distance along the Street of the Armenian Patriarchate, brings you to the **Cathedral of Saint James** and its convent. Visits are allowed to the ancient and mysterious church, but only during afternoon services.

The most direct route from the Jaffa Gate and the Citadel to Temple Mount is by way of the intriguing oriental bazaars along the **Street of David** (as you come through Jaffa Gate, just walk in a straight line to the descending steps). You'll know you're in the right place by the small boys, who hurtle down the narrow street with carts full of vegetables, bolts of cloth, leather goods and sides of mutton. The carts serve shops in the places where larger vehicles can't go; their only brakes are old tires dragged by chains, which the boys step on before the speed becomes murderous.

The **bazaar** is simply fascinating. Souvenir shops abound, their façades draped with carpets and cloths, their interiors piled high with treasures and trash. After examining the glitter and gimcrackery, don't miss a look in the many local shops which give the bazaar much of its character. Spice shops are filled with brimming sacks of fragrant powders and seeds, and at the butcher's your eyes will meet those of a dozen disembodied sheeps' heads, ready for the pot. Tailors, cobblers and metalworkers all ply their trades near the din of hagglers in the municipal produce market. Trying to distinguish the various smells can be fascinating: the spice shops exude a symphony of them, and you'll also meet with the odour of frying *falafel* (a spiced paste of chick-peas), the aroma of freshly ground coffee, of scented wood being worked at the joiner's, and the rich and acrid smoke of hashish, tolerated among the local people but taboo to foreigners. At many places along the Street of David you can stop for a soft drink or a refreshing glass of fruit juice.

The street leads right, then left into the Street of the Chain (HaShalshelet, Es-Silsila), which goes straight for the Bab es-Silsila, the Gate of the Chain. This is only one of several entrances to the Haram es-Sharif, the "noble enclosure" atop Temple Mount. You can visit Temple Mount daily, but on Friday, the Moslem

Sabbath, and major Moslem holidays the Haram is closed to non-Moslems. (During the holy month of Ramadan special rules apply.)

Temple Mount, or Mount Moriah, where King Solomon built the First Temple and later generations the Second, is holy ground to all three of Jerusalem's great religions. So sacred are the confines of the Temple site that strictly observant Jews dare not even come here, and Moslems and Chris-

Traditional transport is still best in narrow, congested Old City.

tians come with great reverence. Solomon's Temple was completed in about 960 B.C., but the Babylonians destroyed it 400 years later. By 515 B.C., Jews under the rule of Cyrus of Persia had built the Second Temple. It was to last for 600 years until it was destroyed by the Romans.

For Moslems, ever since Mo- **25**

hammed stepped upon the rock on Temple Mount, which tradition identifies as Abraham's altar, the place has been El-Haram es-Sharif. The Prophet made the mysterious night-time journey accompanied by a band of angels, mounted upon El-Burak, a miraculous beast. Built right over the celebrated rock in 691, the **Dome of the Rock** (Kubbet es-Sakhra) is Jerusalem's most strikingly beautiful house of worship. Panels of brilliantly coloured tiles and bands of Koranic inscriptions surround the upper part of the octagonal mosque, while marble panels in muted pastel shades offset this brilliance from below. Leave your shoes by the door as you enter.

The richness of the exterior decoration is echoed, even excelled, inside. The rock is surrounded by a richly worked wooden screen, and above it are stained-glass windows and black-and-gold mosaics simply breathtaking in their beauty. Look carefully at the rock to find Mohammed's footprint, and inspect the small tabernacle at its southern extremity, which holds several hairs from

Monument to a miraculous flight: Dome of the Rock blazes with gold and polychrome tilework.

the Prophet's beard. The sacred rock has a secret, too, for down a few steps and underneath it is a grotto where, so they say, great prophets and kings of the past came to pray, and the souls of the dead travel for their devotions.

Surrounding the Dome of the Rock are smaller Islamic buildings put up at different times. The **Dome of the Chain** is a miniature copy of the Dome of the Rock. Sabeel Qait Bey, an ornate little 15th-century kiosk, shows the fine sense of design and craftsmanship of the Mameluke period. From it, fresh water was served to mosque visitors in earlier times. By the arches and stairs leading down to El-Aksa Mosque is the pretty Minber of Kadi Burhan ed-Din, a summer pulpit used in warm weather when prayers can be said outdoors.

Pass under the arches and down the steps to El-Aksa Mosque. Note the sundial at the centre top of the archway. It's accurate to within about five minutes of correct time, and has the advantage of needing no winding, though it does seem to "stop" on cloudy days.

Further down, you pass two places reserved for the ritual ablutions which must be performed by Moslems before prayers. One is a circular fountain with a pool, fitted at the bottom with spigots and seats and called El-Kas ("The Cup").

The caliph El-Walid built the first **El-Aksa** (715) on the site of an earlier holy place but earthquakes destroyed it. In 1034 it was rebuilt, basically in the form it has today. The Crusaders used it as a church, but when Saladin conquered Jerusalem, El-Aksa became a mosque once more.

The structure is imposing from the outside, and its grandeur affects you even more once you've slipped off your shoes and entered the great cool interior. Mammoth marble pillars support beams and a ceiling painted in coloured arabesques; the floor is graced by oriental carpets with ever more intricate patterns. Stained-glass windows, worshippers at prayer, and a holy man reading to himself from the Koran add to the calm and peaceful atmosphere. Be careful not to walk in front of those at prayer. At the far end of the mosque the pillars are of precious breccia and chalcedony and the stone work in the *mihrab* (prayer niche) has delicate carvings.

East of El-Aksa is a large open pavement, underneath which lie tremendous vaulted

chambers called Solomon's Stables. You will have to find a guide and pay an extra fee to visit this dingy, man-made cavern. From the far eastern corner in the wall is a marvellous **view** of the Mount of Olives and the Garden of Gethsemane plus the ancient tombs in the Kidron Valley below. Tradition says that this corner is the "Pinnacle of the Temple" where Jesus was brought by Satan during his temptation *(Matt. 4:5).*

El Aksa's opulent interior: the carpets alone are worth a fortune.

Just below the Dome of the Rock and El-Aska is the **Western Wall** ("Wailing Wall") of Temple Mount. Of all places in the world, it is the most revered by Jews. Since the time of the Second Temple's destruction and banishment of the Jews in A.D. 70, Jews have come here to pray and to weep at the loss of the House of God, and to hope for the restitution of Jerusalem to the Jewish people. When that hope was realized in June 1967, old buildings which crowded the Wall were demolished and a wide plaza was constructed to accommodate the hundreds of worshippers who arrived daily. Whatever your beliefs you'll feel a sense of awe when approaching the giant **29**

stone ashlars (blocks) which supported the foundations of the Temple, and which represent for the Jewish people a promise and a dream come true.

The ashlars of the Prayer Place date from the time of Herod the Great, with later constructions of smaller blocks higher up. This is only a small section of the Western Wall, which overall extends from one side of Temple Mount to the other and is sunk deeply in the rubble-filled earth.

Separate sections of the Wall are reserved for male and female worshippers. Men must have head coverings and women must not have bare shoulders or short skirts when entering the enclosure of the Prayer Place. Skull-caps and shawls are lent free of charge to those who need them.

The gate in the city walls nearest Temple Mount has the unusual name of Dung Gate (Shaar HaAshpot), probably due to the activities of the city's waste collection men in ancient times. There's a first aid station along the road just inside the gate.

Giant ashlars fitted with precision recall the Temple's glory.

Bordering the plaza at the Western Wall is Old Jerusalem's **Jewish Quarter,** much damaged during the fighting in 1948. The area was in Jordanian hands until reclaimed by Israeli forces in 1967. Since then, reconstruction has been rapid, with new and distinguished houses, shops and synagogues lining every street. Wandering through the Jewish Quarter on a Saturday is the best way to tiptoe back into its history. Among the ruins, some going back to the 1st century B.C., black-clad Hassidic Jews lead children to synagogue or *yeshivas* (schools) for Sabbath study. No less active on weekdays, the quarter includes a centre for writers called Artists' House, artists' galleries and studios, shops, restaurants and cafés.

The **Ramban Synagogue** on Rehov HaYehudim, is the oldest house of worship still standing in the quarter, and was built by Rabbi Moshe Nahmanides when he reestablished the Jewish community here in 1267. Right next to the Ramban is the **Yehuda He-Hasid Synagogue,** also called HaHurva or Beit Yaakov, built on the ruins of the 13th-century Crusader Church of St. Martin. Rabbi Yehuda led a thousand of his Polish followers to the

Holy City in 1699 and shortly afterwards began construction of the synagogue. Finally completed only in 1864, it was the centre of Ashkenazi worship in the city until the fighting of 1948 when the building was demolished and it became a ruin once more.

The **Yohanan Ben Zakkai Synagogue** is actually four synagogues in one. Finished in 1586, it was the centre of Sephardic worship for centuries. The largest room gives the complex its name. As little decoration was left in these buildings by 1967, furnishings from abandoned Italian synagogues have been used.

The **Tiferet Israel Synagogue,** also called Nisan Bek, was dedicated just over a century ago at a spot off Misgav Ladach and Chayei Olam streets. Though it was not hallowed by time and the prayers of thousands of worshippers like its venerable neighbours, Tiferet Israel was the tallest and perhaps the grandest synagogue in late 19th-century Jerusalem. Destroyed in the 1948 war, it is now being rebuilt.

For a look at what it was like to live in the Jewish Quarter during the 19th century, pay a visit to the **Old Yishuv Court Museum** (see p. 87).

Via Dolorosa and the Moslem Quarter

The Way of the Cross, or Via Dolorosa, holds a fascination for visitors to Jerusalem no matter what their beliefs. Though you can reach the starting-point of the walk along the Stations of the Cross by various routes, a stroll through the Moslem Quarter is a picturesque introduction to the Jerusalem of early Christian times.

Begin at **Damascus Gate** (Shaar Shechem, Bab el-Amud), in the Old City's northern wall, grandest and most impressive of all of Jerusalem's gates. What you see is the work of Suleiman the Magnificent's masons and builders, done in the 16th century. Beggars solicit alms at the city gates as they did in ancient times, and just inside the gate is a centre for Arab money-changers. Don't expect to see glittering heaps of gold and silver or delicately balanced scales, for they've long been replaced by paper notes and pocket calculators.

Medieval grandeur of Damascus Gate dominates northern wall of Old City: can he capture it?

Through the great gate and down a flight of steps brings you into the busy bazaar streets. Take the street called **El-Wad.** Souvenir and jewellery shops are used to catering to foreign tourists so be prepared for some proprietors who seem to look upon it as a special treat whenever a foreigner drops in.

Turn left into the Via Dolorosa and walk along to the eastern end to the **Lions' Gate,** or St. Stephen's Gate, built in Sultan Suleiman's time. Ac-

cording to the legend, the great Sultan was threatened in a dream by two lions who told him to see to the rebuilding of Jerusalem's dilapidated walls. He rebuilt them quickly and magnificently, transferring his visionary antagonists to a place of honour on this handsome gate. Stop for a moment here to admire the **view** of the Kidron Valley, and the Mount of Olives on the other side of it, with the Garden of Gethsemane a green patch on the

mountain slope, and ancient Jewish cemeteries ranged on the slopes to the south.

Back through the gate again brings you to the purest example of Crusader architecture still standing in Jerusalem: the **Church of St. Anne.** Saints Anne and Joachim, parents of the Virgin Mary, lived on this site when Mary was born, and you can visit the grotto beneath the church where St. Anne gave birth. The church itself is plain and stocky. Built

On Mount of Olives' slope, the verdant Garden of Gethsemane.

in Burgundian style, it was finished in 1140 during the reign of Fulk of Anjou, Crusader King of Jerusalem. Before that century was out, Jerusalem had been conquered by Moslem invaders and the church and convent became an Islamic seminary for a time. The buildings crumbled later during centuries of neglect until Napoleon III **35** had the church completely restored in the mid-19th century and presented it to the Order of the White Fathers *(Pères Blancs)*.

Next to St. Anne's are excavations of the **Pool of Bethesda,** where sacrificial sheep were washed before being brought to the Temple, and where Jesus cured the crippled man *(John 5:2–9)*. The lowest level of the pool dates from Hasmonean times; subsequently the Romans built a pagan shrine here, the Byzantines a large church to commemorate Jesus' miracle, and the Crusaders constructed a chapel, all of which were swept away over the centuries—a real microcosm of Jerusalem's history.

After leaving the church rejoin the Via Dolorosa and walk up the street to the Franciscan monastery (the Convent of the Flagellation), starting-point for the walk along the Stations of the Cross.

Franciscan monks have been retracing Jesus' steps and caring for the holy sites along the Via Dolorosa since the 15th century. Walks are usually offered at 9 a.m. and 3 p.m. each day, with the afternoon walk on Fridays being especially well-attended. The Franciscan guide usually speaks English and the tour is free of charge. Check the current bulletin of *Events in the Jerusalem Region* on dates and times of the walk, and then be sure to wait for the Franciscan monk. (Neighbourhood boys, acting as self-appointed guides, may tell you "there's no walk today", but it's better to wait for the Franciscan guide—he shares in the experience accumulated over five hundred years.)

The Stations of the Cross

Some of the events mentioned in the Gospels can still be matched with places along the Via Dolorosa, others are less sure, and a few are almost certainly the stuff of legends. In fact, the 14 stations as they are today were mapped out in the 16th century by European Christians who had never been to Jerusalem, and who used documentary and hearsay evidence—which explains why the legendary stations crept in.

Pilgrims from Europe, who had read these descriptions and followed the stations in their own churches at home, were not content to be shown only four or seven stations by Franciscan monks actually living in Jerusalem. The monks later decided that faith could also be served by changing the plan of the stations to accommodate the pilgrims' pre-formed no-

V: SIMONI CYRENAEO
CRUX IMPONITUR · ST·

Bearing the cross in Jesus'
steps shows special devotion.

tions—thus Europeans' guesses became Jerusalem's "facts".

STATION I (Condemnation): Jesus was condemned in Herod's Antonia Fortress, the site of which is now covered by modern buildings. Tradition has it that Pilate delivered Jesus to his soldiers at a spot now in the courtyard of El-Omariye School, across the street from the Franciscan monastery.

STATION II (Jesus receives the cross): After being condemned, Jesus was taken away by the soldiers, who beat and mocked him in the fortress courtyard, put a crown of thorns on his head and led him away to be crucified *(Mark 15:16–20)*. Much of the fortress courtyard pavement, made of huge flagstones, still exists in the monastery and the Convent of the Sisters of Zion, next door. You can see the pavement, or **37**

Lithostrotos, plus the Franciscans' Chapel of the Flagellation (a medieval building refurnished in 1927) and the Chapel of Condemnation, which are both built upon the Lithostrotos.

Before being given the cross in the courtyard, Jesus was presented to the people by Pilate who said "Behold the man!" *(John 19:5).* The site is likely to have been near the fortress entrance, or somewhat past the arch, built in A.D. 135, which is now named "Ecce Homo Arch".

STATION III (Jesus falls): The Gospels carry no word of this event, but popular tradition has

Convent of the Flagellation: the Via Dolorosa begins at its door.

the Spasm Armenian Catholic Church commemorates the meeting of Mary and Jesus.

STATION V (Simon carries Jesus' cross): In the Gospels, a man from Cyrenaica (modern Libya) was forced by the guard of soldiers to carry the cross *(Matt. 27:32)* when it looked as though Jesus couldn't go on. A small 19th-century Franciscan oratory marks the spot.

STATION VI (Veronica wipes Jesus' face): Your guide will have a door in the wall opened, and you will step down into the little **Church of St. Veronica,** built in the restored vaults of a Crusader monastery. Tradition says a woman wiped the sweaty, bloody face of Jesus here, and an imprint of his visage was left on the cloth. The Latin for "True Image" has given us the name "Veronica", and since the woman's name is unknown she has become St. Veronica. The legend has been a part of Jerusalem lore since the 7th century and the mysterious cloth bearing the image is now kept at St. Peter's in Rome.

STATION VII (Jesus falls again): At the crossroads of the Via Dolorosa and the market street of Khan ez-Zeit is the

it that Jesus fell under the weight of the cross at a spot just around the first corner you come to during the walk. A Polish chapel, with a relief showing Jesus bearing the cross, marks the spot.

STATION IV (Jesus meets his mother): A small shrine near the entrance to Our Lady of

39

spot where, tradition says, Jesus fell under the weight of the cross a second time.

STATION VIII (Jesus speaks to Jerusalem's women): A cross in stone relief on the wall marks the site. St. Luke reports that Jesus stopped along the way to Golgotha and told the women who were following him that they should weep for themselves and their children rather than for him *(Luke 23:28)*. In fact, a mere 36 years after Jesus' crucifixion, Jerusalem was destroyed by Roman troops, its citizens starved, killed in battle, executed or sold into slavery.

STATION IX (Jesus falls a third time): Jesus' third fall under the weight of the cross is according to legend, and therefore the exact location is disputed. Your guide will lead you south along Khan ez-Zeit from Station VIII, up a stairway to the **Ethiopian Convent** on the roof of the Church of the Holy Sepulchre. A bit of column embedded in a wall is now cited as Station IX, though it is of less interest than the convent itself. Sombre and stately Ethiopian monks stride here occupying the curious rooftop settlement, the only part of the church which the Copts, one of the world's oldest Christian communities, can claim.

40 The Way of the Cross now

Holy Sepulchre Church shelters Golgotha and Jesus' tomb, most sacred spots in Christendom.

leads into the **Church of the Holy Sepulchre** itself, which shelters the five final Stations. There has been a Church of the Holy Sepulchre on this spot for some 1,650 years, ever since Queen Helena visited Jerusalem and identified the site of Golgotha* in A.D. 326. Emperor Constantine the Great then had a tremendous and magnificent basilica and rotunda built to house the tomb of Jesus. This, the grandest and richest of all churches to stand here, was destroyed in the year 614 by invading Persians. It was later rebuilt, but the form it has today dates mostly from Crusader times.

The plan of the church seems to have been drawn more by history than by a single architect, and bickering among clergy of the various sects over rights within the church has added to the confusion. Disagreement over who governs what was so bad in the 19th century that the sultan had to step in, and Jerusalem wit-

---

* The hill where Jesus was crucified was skull-shaped. The names "Golgotha" and "Calvary" derive from Hebrew and Latin words meaning "skull".

nessed the unexpected scene of a Moslem Turkish ruler adjudicating a Christian dispute.

The portal by which visitors enter the church dates from Crusader times (1149). The western door of the pair is open: the eastern door was bricked up a few years after the church's completion and has stayed that way ever since.

STATION X (Jesus is stripped): Immediately on stepping into the church, turn right and climb the narrow staircase. The platform here rests partly on the rock of Golgotha itself. The soldiers stripped Jesus of his clothes, which they later divided among themselves (*Matt. 27:35*), at this spot near where the cross was placed.

STATION XI (Jesus is nailed to the cross): The Franciscan chapel on the platform—the one to the right—is traditionally where Jesus was nailed to the cross.

STATION XII (Jesus' death): To the left of the Franciscan chapel is a Greek Orthodox altar, profusely decorated and attended by a black-robed priest. He will show you a hole under the altar, and a small silver disc marking the place where, tradition says, Jesus' cross was set up, with those of the two thieves on either side.

STATION XIII (Jesus is taken down from the cross): Between the Franciscan and Greek altars is a small shrine with an ancient wooden figure of Mary in a glass case. In the Gospels, Mary was present at Jesus' death (*John 19:26*).

Take the right-hand stairs down from the platform to the ground floor, and just in front of you will be the Stone of the Unction where Jesus' body was anointed with spices and myrrh and then interred a few steps away in Joseph of Arimathea's personal tomb.

STATION XIV (The Holy Sepulchre): Joseph of Arimathea, a follower of Jesus, donated the tomb, which was a two-room crypt cut in the rock of Golgotha. Most of the rock was cut away with the construction of earlier Churches of the Holy Sepulchre; all that remains is the stone shelf on which Jesus' body lay, now covered in polished marble. The present structure (aedicule) enclosing the tomb was designed by an Orthodox architect in the 19th century. The tiny chamber in which Jesus was buried can hold only six people at a time and you may have a few minutes' wait.

In the Church of the Holy Sepulchre itself there's plenty of room for moving around. Over the centuries each corner

Station XIII: Mary wept as Jesus' body was removed from the cross.

and nook has taken on some significance, and small chapels have been dedicated to the different people and events related to Jesus' crucifixion and resurrection. Just opposite the entrance to the aedicule is the **Greek Orthodox Katholikon,** a brilliantly decorated nave only recently restored to its original splendour.

If you stand facing the aedicule with your back to the Katholikon, the Franciscan chapel of Mary Magdalene will be on your right. This is the spot where, according to tradition, Mary Magdalene discovered the resurrection of Jesus. A Franciscan convent, seminary and church are grouped around the chapel.

Mount Zion

Directly south of the Old City, just outside the walls, is Mount Zion. Few places in the world can claim equal significance with this barren Judean hilltop, revered by millions and visited by hundreds daily. Leaving the Old City, you pass through Zion Gate which is pitted with bullet holes from the modern wars which have raged around it. For a good look at Mount Zion, the Old City, and surrounding Judean hills, take a walk along the top of the walls near Zion Gate. Stairways and railings just inside the gate make it safe.

Mount Zion is dominated by the **Dormition Abbey** of the Benedictine monks. Coming from Zion Gate, bear right to reach the monastery entrance, but note that no visits are allowed between 1 and 3 p.m. Less than a century old, the abbey is a mixture of ancient styles and modern construction. The sanctuary has beautiful gold and polychrome mosaics in the Byzantine style,

Dormition Abbey is Mount Zion's Romanesque crown. Legend says Mary went to heaven from here.

but the abbey's spiritual centre is beneath the sanctuary, in the crypt. An effigy of the Virgin Mary marks the spot where she is said to have spent her last days on earth before her assumption into heaven.

On the opposite side of the Dormition Abbey from its entrance are two more sites of great religious significance. In a tiny low-ceiling room in one of the buildings is the **Tomb of King David.** A guard will provide men with head-coverings, in order to visit. Directly above the tomb, in the same building, is the **Coenaculum** ("dining room") believed to be the place where Jesus and his disciples shared the Last Supper, in celebration of the first night of Passover. The Crusaders built the Gothic archwork, and Turkish rulers of Jerusalem added a prayer niche and inscriptions. It's a small and humble room, hardly the grand hall depicted in Leonardo da Vinci's famous painting.

Before you leave Mount Zion, pay a visit to the **Chamber of the Martyrs,** beneath the other buildings on the Mount, which commemorates the sacrifice of millions of Jewish lives in the Nazi holocaust. The plaques on the walls give the names of the communities which were destroyed.

Mount of Olives

The best way to pay a visit to the Mount of Olives is to take a bus (No. 75 to Et-Tur, from the East Jerusalem bus station) or taxi to the top of the Mount, visit the points of interest there, and then walk down the hillside through the Jewish cemeteries and the Garden of Gethsemane to the Kidron Valley.

Driving through the valley called Wadi el-Guz or Nahal Egoz and up the slopes of the Mount of Olives takes you past the Augusta Victoria Hospital, and, after turning at the crest of the hill, the Greek church of Viri Galilei ("Men of Galilee") is on the right. Farther along is the imposing tower of the Russian Church of the Ascension. The tower's top is the highest point in the city and appropriately it marks the spot from which, according to Orthodox Russian belief, Jesus ascended to heaven. The nuns in the convent here preserve their seclusion, and visitors must have special permission.

Most other Christian denominations accept the **Chapel of the Ascension** as the place of Jesus' ascension. Down the road from the Russian church, the dome is now in the grounds of a little mosque. The modest structure is built over a rock **45** said to be the last upon which Jesus stood. Don't expect a breathtaking architectural masterpiece when you visit the chapel; despite its significance, it's very plain.

Near the Chapel of the Ascension you'll find relief for weary feet. Several camel-drivers always wait around the mosque entrance and will be glad to order their huge beasts to kneel down so that you can climb on easily. Depending on how much you're prepared to pay, they will trot you down to the Intercontinental Hotel, or just wait while you have your photo taken.

Just south of the chapel is the **Pater Noster Church,** thought to be built on the spot where Jesus taught his disciples the Lord's Prayer. The present church dates from the late 19th century. Inside, wall decorations include the Lord's Prayer in dozens of languages. In the same compound you'll find the Basilica of Eleona, finished in 1923 on the site of a Byzantine church.

From the Pater Noster church compound, a road heads to Bethphage, traditional starting-point for Jesus' triumphal ride into Jerusalem on the first Palm Sunday. Some ancient Jewish tombs nearby help to conjure up a vivid picture of what the area looked like two thousand years ago.

A short distance along the main road from Pater Noster Church is the Intercontinental Hotel, and in front of it an observation point for the breathtaking **view** of Old Jerusalem. A small amphitheatre provides a convenient place to sit down and take it all in. Looking across the Kidron Valley, one's eye is immediately drawn to the sheen of the golden Dome of the Rock and its brilliantly coloured tiles. The eastern city wall, with a Moslem graveyard at its foot, is broken by the impressive grace of the **Golden Gate** (also called Mercy Gate or Eternal Gate). The gate has been walled in for centuries, and many believe it will not be reopened until the Messiah appears and enters Jerusalem. The Byzantines built the splendid gate on the ruins of earlier ones; the Crusaders added and embellished it in the 12th century, and Sultan Suleiman repaired it in the 16th. The Lions' (St. Stephen's) Gate is to the right of Golden Gate.

Scanning the ancient and sacred city from the Mount of Olives, it's easy to see why so many devout people of different religions regard Mount Zion as the place where the

Messiah will make his presence known. Looking from north to south, the hill stands out at the far end, crowned by the conical roof of the Dormition Abbey. This sweeping vista of Jerusalem has changed greatly over the centuries, but has never failed to stir the souls of the countless pilgrims who have made the long journey to the Holy Land.

North along the road from the observation point, a narrow road descends into the extensive Jewish cemeteries on the slope, the oldest and largest in the world. Some graves go back to biblical times. The pebbles placed on top symbolize a visit by a devoted mourner. Just off the downward road are the **Tombs of the Prophets,** sombre rock-hewn tunnels carved with burial niches said to contain the remains of Zechariah, Haggai, Malachi and many others.

Descending the hill, the 19th-century church of **Dominus Flevit** ("The Lord Wept") commemorates Jesus' weeping over Jerusalem (*Luke 19:41–42*). During construction, artefacts, tombs and ruins from many periods of Jerusalem's history were uncovered, some dating from late Bronze Age times (about 1600 B.C.).

The **Garden of Gethsemane**

occupies the lower part of the slope, and various parts are cared for by different sects. The **Russian Orthodox Church** of Mary Magdalene with its gilded onion-shaped domes is in the first part of the garden. The exquisite church was built by order of Tsar Alexander III and his brothers in memory of their mother. Entering the church's one large room, your eye is immediately caught by the marvellously smooth and lustrous white marble of the iconostasis. The body of the Russian Grand Duchess Elizabeth reposes in the church's crypt. Russian Orthodox nuns oversee the church and its grounds.

On the lower reaches of the slope of the Mount of Olives, leading on to the Jericho Road, is the **Basilica of the Agony,** also called the Church of all Nations, the tympanum of its façade shining with brilliant mosaic work. In the mosaic scene, Christ weeps as he prays in Gethsemane (*Luke 22:41–45*). The church was built on the site of Byzantine and Crusader ruins, paid for by donations from people all over the world, and dedicated by the Franciscans in 1924. You may notice curious glass plates in the church floor: they allow you to see fragments of the Byzantine **47** floor mosaics left from the earlier church.

The highlight of a visit to the Basilica is a walk in the garden, filled with cacti, century plants and bougainvillea. The garden also harbours some gnarled and venerable olive trees. They say an olive tree never dies but sprouts new wood when an old trunk is decrepit: hence these ancient fellows may have been there when Jesus walked in the garden. "Gethsemane" comes from the Hebrew *Geth-shemna*, meaning "oilpress".

A few steps from the Basilica of the Agony, at the head of the Kidron Valley, is **Mary's Tomb.** Through an attractive Crusader arch, stairs lead down a long and dingy passageway to the Orthodox Church of the Assumption. At the bottom, in the gloomy subterranean church, is a rock-hewn sepulchre. Hundreds of smoky, scented votive lamps hang from the ceiling and give off a dull gleam. Some traditions give this as the place of Mary's burial and assumption into heaven, though the Dormition Abbey on Mount Zion also claims the honour.

The Franciscan **Grotto of Gethsemane,** entered by turning right before reaching the Crusader arch, is a less sombre place. Jesus may well have

gathered here with his disciples during the years of his teaching; visits are allowed during the same hours as at the Basilica of the Agony.

In Jerusalem, every stone and every structure has its significance. The little Moslem shrine by the roadway near Mary's Tomb is actually the

Jesus may well have knelt beneath this ancient Gethsemane olive tree.

grave of the 15th-century Moslem judge and historian Mujr ed-Din. Nearby, at the head of the Kidron Valley, the Greek Orthodox Church of St. Stephen commemorates the first Christian martyr *(Acts 7:59–60).* And up the Jericho Road toward the city is a small but dramatic monument to Israeli soldiers killed in the 1967 Six-Day War.

The Kidron Valley
(Valley of Jehoshaphat)

The valley between Temple Mount and the Mount of Olives holds traces left by the men who inhabited this area in earliest times. The original settlement of Jerusalem, founded perhaps around 3000 B.C., was on the western side of this valley, and tombs and monuments have been built here ever since.

Gravestones with crosses and Arabic inscriptions at the head of the valley remind foreign visitors that many Arabs are Christians. Most of the graves are recent, barely a century old, but the striking, time-worn monument seen down the valley is thought to date from the Second Temple period over two thousand years ago. Legend says it is the **Tomb of Absalom.** Behind it is the smaller Tomb of Jehoshaphat, dating from the same period.

Though many legends are connected with the next set of tombs farther on, an inscription on them sets us right. The Tomb of Bnei Hezir was carved in Greek style from the rock of the valley wall for a Jewish priestly family (the Sons of Hezir) of the 2nd century B.C. Whether or not St. James ever took refuge or was buried here, as Christian tradition says,

we may never know for certain.

A four-sided pyramid tops the **Tomb of Zechariah,** dating from about the time of Jesus. No one is quite sure which Zechariah is buried here: is it Zechariah the prophet (who is also said to be interred in the Tombs of the Prophets, up the hill), or Zechariah the father of John the Baptist?

Gazing up to the south-eastern corner of the city walls, you are actually looking at the site of King David's city, which would have been a tiny village by today's standards. It occupied the slope of the hill south of El-Aksa Mosque, called the Ophel, or City of David, and modern excavations have brought to light bits of wall from the City of David and its successors. The settlement was situated here partly because the Gihon spring, in a cavern just to the west of the modern road, provided plenty of water. The spring lay outside the city walls in ancient times, and is the same source for which the Jebusites constructed their tunnel (see p. 12). In 701 B.C., King Hezekiah had another tunnel dug, which led to the **Pool of Siloam,** which was within the

Zechariah's Tomb is cloaked in mystery; above are smaller tombs.

city walls south-west of the Gihon. Under siege by the ferocious Assyrians, the king and his people quaffed the cool water of Gihon to their hearts' content while the Assyrians sat with parched throats. The triumphant Israelite sappers who dug the tunnel left an inscription in it to celebrate its completion; it was discovered in 1880 while Jerusalem was an Ottoman city, and the tablet on which it was inscribed is now in the Museum of the Ancient Orient in Istanbul.

Long after King Hezekiah drank from the waters of Gihon, legend says that the Virgin Mary brought her infant son's clothes here to wash them. The Pool of Siloam, moreover, has its own reputation as the place where Jesus restored sight to a blind man *(John 9:6–7)*. A church was once built over this spot, but today the minaret of a small mosque is the best landmark for finding the pool.

The lower reaches of the Kidron Valley are now filled by the Arab town of SILWAN, which is known to be built over parts of ancient Jewish graveyards. The town tumbles down the southern end of the Mount of Olives, known here as the "Mount of Offence", having acquired a disreputable name in the time of Solomon.

The great king built altars to pagan gods worshipped by his non-Jewish wives on this slope, a terrible offence against the God of Israel *(1 Kings 11:1–12)*. Today nothing remains of those ill-founded altars.

East Jerusalem

Though Jerusalem was reunited after the Six-Day War in 1967, the parts earlier held by Jordan retain their Arab way of life. East Jerusalem has its modern streets and ancient monuments just as West Jerusalem does, and because East and West were separate cities in earlier years, you will find a Central Post Office, bus station, YMCA, and even consulates duplicated in both parts of the city.

The Arabs of East Jerusalem, whether Christian or Moslems, warmly welcome foreign visitors of all religions as they have for centuries. (From 1948 to 1967 all pilgrims stayed in East Jerusalem hotels and visited shrines in the Old City, then part of East Jerusalem.)

If you are not staying in one of East Jerusalem's hotels, plan for at least a morning's visit to this part of the city, perhaps with a return in the evening for an Arabic dinner and an oriental show. Note carefully the

change in Sabbaths: the Moslem Arabs have Friday as their day of rest, beginning at sunset on Thursday and lasting until sunset on Friday. Shops are closed and restaurants may not be serving alcoholic drinks during this time.

A good place to begin your wanderings is Damascus Gate.

The preoccupation of many Jerusalem citizens: thoughtful study.

Walk north on the Nablus Road (Derech Shechem) and look for a lane on the right with a sign pointing the way to the **Garden Tomb.** General Gordon, British hero of China and **53**

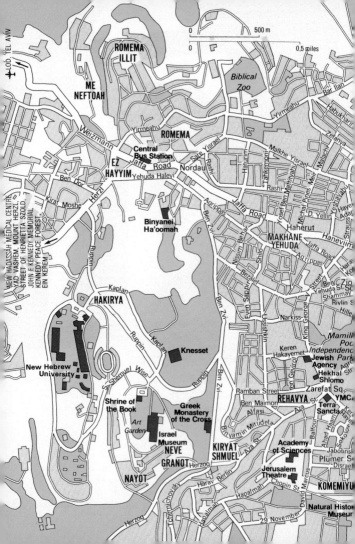

CENTRAL JERUSALEM

Khartoum, visited Jerusalem in 1883 on his way back to Egypt and found that this rock-hewn cave fitted very well the description of Jesus' tomb. A skull-like hill is close by, and a vision one night strengthened Gordon's belief in the authenticity of the place. An association of British Protestants owns and maintains the attractive grounds and gardens, and welcomes all visitors. Whether this is truly Jesus' burial-place or not, the tomb is "unspoiled" compared to the one in the Church of the Holy Sepulchre.

At the intersection of the Nablus Road and Saladin Street, you are in the midst of the quarter called the American Colony, after a late 19th-century group of benefactors who started a suburb here when Jerusalem was beginning to emerge from the ancient city walls. The imposing church tower is that of St. George's Anglican Cathedral, seat of the Anglican Archbishop of Jerusalem and of a school and seminary. You may stroll into the "close" if the gates are open.

Just east of the intersection, in Saladin Street, is the entrance to the eerie **Tombs of the Kings,** misnamed at first and later found to be the 1st-century B.C. tomb of Queen Helena of Adiabne, in Mes-

opotamia. As you wander in and begin to descend the broad, rough-hewn staircase, a guide from the caretaker's family may catch up with you and point out the tomb's curiosities: grooves cut in the rock walls to catch rainwater and convey it to cisterns, the rolling stone door which sealed the tomb, and the burial niches themselves, spooky and foreboding in the dim light of the guide's tiny candle flame. At the end of the tour your guide will politely re-

quest a tip, and will suggest a figure many times greater than he actually expects to receive.

Continuing down the hill along the Nablus Road takes you past the gracious American Colony Hotel, once the palace of a Turkish pasha, to the small Sheikh Jarrah Mosque which gives this part of the city its name. Past the mosque, turn right, and then left, to reach the **Tomb of Simon the Just** (Shimeon Hazadik), a high priest during the Second

Sepulchres like the Garden Tomb were common during Jesus' time.

Temple period. Orthodox Jews hold the site sacred, though an inscription attributes the grave to a Roman owner. As this is Jerusalem, both accounts of the tomb's ownership may be true.

North-east of Simon's Tomb, **Mount Scopus** rises and surveys all of Jerusalem, old and new. From 1948 to 1967 this was an Israeli enclave **57**

within East Jerusalem. The Hebrew University and the Hadassah Medical Centre were active here before 1948. They had to be closed down during partition, but are again in operation today. The Harry Truman Research Institute is the most striking of the new buildings. The university library serves as Israel's National Library as well. You'll need to go by car, taxi or bus to reach the heights of the Mount.

Take some time to admire the view of the Judean hills and desert from the **amphitheatre** built into the hillside. Even better, come for an open-air concert here on a summer's evening.

On your return to the centre of East Jerusalem from Mount Scopus, you will pass the British War Cemetery of the soldiers who fell fighting for Jerusalem in 1917, yet another reminder of the city's turbulent history. You can also make a diversion to the **Tombs of the**

Sanhedrin, the supreme rabbinical court of Second Temple times. The impressive rock-hewn tombs are in the quarter called Sanhedria.

Retracing your steps from Simon's Tomb to St. George's, take Saladin Street to explore the central area of East Jerusalem's modern business district, perhaps stopping at a sidewalk stand for a soft drink and a *kayek* (pronounced KAH-yek, from the English "cake"), an oval-shaped bread roll

Traditional life-styles are the soul of Jerusalem (Mount Scopus).

sprinkled with sesame seeds. At the end of Saladin Street are the city walls and Herod's Gate, part of Sultan Suleiman's construction, though resting on even more ancient foundations. Herod's Gate remained closed for centuries, but was reopened in 1875 as the city expanded.

Across Sultan Suleiman Street from Herod's Gate is the **59**

Rockefeller Museum (see p. 86) perched on a hill. John D. Rockefeller Jr. gave the money to build the museum in 1927. The plot of land chosen as the site gives it a lofty position—right in the path of hundreds of bullets during the 1967 war, as you'll notice by the pitted surface of its stone exterior.

Two more curiosities exist in this area, both underground. Find the bus station on Sultan Suleiman Street between Nablus Road and Saladin Street. A narrow alley runs along the eastern edge of the station lot to a rocky outcrop. Within the outcrop—which is actually the "Skull Hill" of the Garden Tomb—is a cave called Jeremiah's Grotto, from a tradition that the Prophet Jeremiah wrote the Book of Lamentations here and was then laid to rest.

On the opposite side of Sultan Suleiman Street from the grotto, signs direct visitors to a garden and the entrance to **Solomon's Quarries,** from which the stone used to build Second Temple Jerusalem was cut. No place in Jerusalem is free of legend, and this cavern is also known as "Zedekiah's Cave", from a story that King Zedekiah and his army escaped from a siege of Jerusalem in 587 B.C. via this route.

West Jerusalem

West of Damascus Gate and the Nablus Road is the Jerusalem which is the capital city of Israel. In the early years of the State of Israel, government offices were set up in the central business district, but now the capital and the government have grown, and are spread over many Judean hilltops. You can easily tour the centre of modern Jerusalem on foot, while the outlying districts are served by city buses and taxis.

Starting-point for a walk in West Jerusalem is **Zahal Square,** at the westernmost corner of the Old City walls. In the late 19th century, the growth of modern Jerusalem was so great that the Ottoman monarch, Sultan Abdul Hamid II, decided to open a new gate in the city walls to serve the new colonies to the west. The result was New Gate (1887), a few steps north-east of the square.

Just across the street from New Gate is the enormous hospice and monastery of Notre Dame de Jerusalem, built in the same year as New Gate. Once administered by the Augustinian Fathers of the Assumption, it is now a hostel for pilgrims.

Across Jaffa Road from the

Central Post Office are buildings now housing the Law Courts, but which were at one time part of the **Russian Compound,** a walled area built up at the end of the 1800s to house, feed and care for 10,000 Russian pilgrims all at once. Turn right after passing the Law Courts for a look at the compound's huge, green-domed church.

Continuing north-east on Jaffa Road soon brings you to **Zion Square** in the heart of West Jerusalem's centre. From the square you can continue along Jaffa Road to reach the marketplace of **Makhane Yehuda,** often crowded with

As a young sabra (child born in Israel), you're at the centre of world affairs. West Jerusalem's cafes are alive with political talk.

Mea She'arim

Since the times of the biblical Pharisees many groups of Orthodox Jews have tried to rigorously observe the tenets of Hebrew religious law. The quarter called Mea She'arim, north of Zion Square, is the home of Orthodox communities which live the strictly religious life. Signs warn visitors to dress modestly—women must have heads and shoulders covered and wear longish skirts (no trousers), and men should have head coverings. The Sabbath brings a halt to all work here, even the driving of cars, as families flock to the many small synagogues which preserve traditions from around the world. Though you are free to wander through Mea She'arim as you wish, be careful to observe the customs of the quarter and you will find the residents friendly and helpful. The best way to visit the synagogues is to sign up for the excellent **synagogue tour** arranged by the city's travel agencies. The guide is a former resident of the quarter, and knows all the customs, traditions and fascinating back streets of Mea She'arim.

In Mea She'arim, life is lived to the letter of biblical law; religious duties are foremost.

Orthodox Jewish shoppers. The activity is greatest on Fridays before the Sabbath or before the high holidays, and an old-time spirit from eastern Europe prevails. Farther along Jaffa Road, Jerusalem's Central Bus Station has services to all parts of the city and country. You'll find Binyanei Ha'oomah, Jerusalem's convention and exhibition centre capable of accommodating some 3,500 people, in this area.

Another direction to take from Zion Square is along **Ben Yehuda Street**, lined with shops and offices and partially closed to cars in warm weather so that pedestrians can stroll at their leisure. Several open-air cafés flourish on the upper reaches of the street, and are particularly lively in the late afternoon and early evening.

At the top of Ben Yehuda Street, turn left into King George V Street. Farther down is the semi-circular headquarters of the Jewish Agency. Keren Hayesod (United Israel Appeal) and Keren Kayemet (Jewish National Fund) also have offices here. Just past the Jewish Agency compound, at the corner of Agron Ramban and Aza Streets, rises the bold and massive façade of **Hekhal Shlomo,** seat of the chief Rabbis, both **63**

Sephardic and Ashkenazi, of Israel. You can enter to see museum exhibits of ceremonial objects, biblical dioramas, and the complete interior of an 18th-century Paduan synagogue.

On the other side of King George V Street is Jerusalem's **Independence Park.** The Mamilla Pool, near a small Moslem cemetery at the eastern end of the park, is thought to be part of the Old City's ancient water system. Wander through the refreshing greenery of the park to the intersection of Agron, King David and Mamilla Streets, and climb the hill along King David Street past the modern campus of Hebrew Union College. Soon the oriental tower of the **YMCA** will loom above your head on the right. This landmark was built in 1933, and contains the city's first swimming pool. The **view** over Jerusalem from the top of the building's 150-foot tower is magnificent.

The imposing bulk of the **King David Hotel** (1930) is across the street from the YMCA. It was the city's first grand hotel. The entire south wing was blown up by bombs in 1946 when the hotel was used as a gathering-place for British Protectorate personnel, but was later reconstructed.

Again walking south on King David Street, watch for signs pointing the way to **Herod's Family Tomb,** where members of the king's family were interred in rock-cut tombs. Herod himself was buried elsewhere.

At Plumer Square, you are at the centre of a district of fine gardens. Make your way to that curious and completely unexpected structure looming a short distance away: a true-to-life stone **windmill.** The mill and the quarter around it were built in the mid-1800s through the generosity of Jewish Jerusalem's greatest 19th-century patron, Sir Moses Montefiore. The English philanthropist visited the city several times, and financed the construction of Mishkenot Shaananim, a row of dwellings built to encourage Jews to move from dilapidated houses within the walls to more modern and healthy places. Near to Mishkenot Shaananim you'll find the **Yemin Moshe Quarter:** it's not only architecturally captivating, but also harbours many interesting art galleries and craft shops.

Israeli soldiers face danger daily as they patrol the city; but the job has its moments.

Farther Out

Farther west from Zion Square, but still accessible by city bus (No. 9), are many more points of interest. The **Knesset,** Israel's parliament, meets in an attractive modern building on a hilltop and you can tour the legislators' domain. Bring your passport or identity card. As you alight from the bus, look first at the attractive giant **menorah** (seven-branched candelabrum) opposite the Knesset entrance, a present from the Mother of Parliaments.

Amid the modern and often daring architecture of this area is the ancient **Greek Monastery of the Cross,** over a thousand years old. If we can believe the legends, the trees which once grew here were planted by Lot after he fled Sodom, and one of them was later used to fashion Jesus' cross.

Spread along the hillside above the Monastery of the Cross are the chambers of the great **Israel Museum,** actually four museums in one (see p. 85). On the next hilltop to the west is the Hebrew University's new campus (1954), a sprawling collection of buildings constructed after the original campus on Mount Scopus was surrounded in 1948.

Even farther west are sever-al impressive monuments to 20th-century people and events that changed the world. **Mount Herzl** is named after the Austro-Hungarian writer and founder of Zionism whose work aided the eventual establishment of the State of Israel (see p. 18). Herzl's tomb is here, plus a small museum, and in the attractive gardens nearby lie other modern Israeli leaders, including Prime Ministers Levi Eshkol and Golda Meir.

Not far from Mount Herzl is **Yad Vashem** on the Mount of Remembrance, dedicated to the memory of the millions of Jews murdered by the Nazis. Memorials, a documentation centre and a terrifying but effective exhibit showing the horrors of Nazism fill the hilltop and fascinate visitors, who leave Yad Vashem saddened but somehow strengthened as well.

Onward from Yad Vashem the road divides, the lower part leading to the village of Ein Kerem, while the upper one goes to Hadassah Medical Centre. **Ein Kerem** is thought to be the village in which John the Baptist was born, and St. John's Church is said to be on the site of his childhood home. Mary visited the village and Mary's Fountain (also named the "Spring of the Vineyard") is

Memorial to concentration camp victims reminds and pleads: never again.

commemorated by a mosque, a Russian Orthodox convent, and the Franciscan Church of the Visitation resting on Crusader church ruins.

The upper road to **Hadassah** **Medical Centre** has several names, but as you approach the hospital it becomes the Street of Henrietta Szold, named after the founder of Hadassah, the Organization of American

Women Zionists. Marc Chagall was commissioned to design the **windows** in the hospital's small synagogue, and many visitors come to admire the dramatic designs and jewel-like colours of the dozen small windows, each signifying one of the twelve tribes.

Five miles past Hadassah Medical Centre is the large and attractive **Kennedy Memorial** resembling a tree stump and symbolizing a life cut off in its prime. An eternal flame inside, and the Kennedy Peace Forest surrounding the hill, commemorate the former president of the United States and his brother, Robert Kennedy.

Twentieth-century tributes: swirling colours of brilliant Chagall windows, and a simple memorial to two great friends of Israel.

Excursions

On the Road to the Desert

The biblical town of Bethlehem, on the outskirts of Jerusalem, is accessible by city bus from East Jerusalem. On the way, stop for a look at the Tomb of Rachel on the main road. Rachel, mother of Benjamin in the times of the Book of Genesis, is revered by Jew, Christian and Moslem alike, and as a famous mother is especially sought out by women who come to this simple tomb to pray for fertility.

Bethlehem is spread dramatically along the tops of the Judean hills, its church towers and minarets stretching across the sky. The population, mostly Arab, is divided between Christians and Moslems. Manger Square, busy with taxis and tour buses, is right in front of the **Church of the Nativity.** One of the oldest in the world, it has seen many changes since Constantine had it built in 325. You enter through a small, low door, so designed to keep potential aggressors from riding straight in. The church is situated above the Grotto of the Nativity, a

small subterranean chamber in which a silver star marks the place of Jesus' birth. A side chapel is said to be where the manger stood. The Church of the Nativity, like the Church of the Holy Sepulchre, is divided into zones of possession among the various Christian sects, but the visitor is free to wander from one to the other.

On the road south towards Hebron, your eye will catch a strange hill of conical appearance, off to the east. This is the

Candles have steadily burned in the Church of the Nativity for over sixteen hundred years.

Herodium, a stupendous 300-foot-high artificial mountain built by order of Herod the Great and once topped with lavish palaces, defensive towers and lofty battlements. King Herod was later buried in his awesome creation.

The road from Bethlehem to Hebron passes by Solomon's Pools, three large reservoirs in a shady grove which helped supply Jerusalem, some 13 kilometres away, with water via an aqueduct. The black, free-form shapes of Bedouin tents show up here and there along the road, and many more encampments are hidden behind hills, out of sight of the road. This is the Wilderness of Judah.

The town of **Hebron** is very, very old, attested to by the Cave of Makhpelah, containing the **Tombs of the Patriarchs.** Beneath this fortress-like structure in the centre of town, now covered by a mosque, lie the remains of Abraham, Isaac and Jacob, and of their wives Sarah, Rebecca and Leah. The tombs are in the cave within the building's Herodian foundations. "Memorial tombs", not containing remains, serve as centres for devotions by Jews, Christians and Moslems. The **mosque,** once a Crusader church, is graced with beautiful Mameluke stone and mosaic work, some of the finest Islamic decoration to be seen in Israel. A side chapel, or "Women's Mosque", is said to contain the tomb of Joseph, who was sold into slavery by his brothers, later to return home as Viceroy of Egypt. Rights to visit the mosque above the tombs are shared, with different times for Moslems and non-Moslems.

Some 45 kilometres south of Hebron, on the edge of the desert, lies **Beersheba** (Well of the Oath). About 4,000 years ago Abraham dug a well here, but little of importance happened until 1948 when the town sprang to life. Today, Beersheba has over 100,000 inhabitants, many of them new immigrants who have come to help make the desert bloom and reap its natural wealth.

Be sure to visit Beersheba on a Wednesday and stay the night so you can get up early on Thursday morning for the picturesque **camel market,** which starts at 6 a.m. and is almost finished by 9 a.m. Despite its name, the camel market is the scene of buying and selling all kinds of other things as well: carpets and handicrafts, souvenirs and daily necessities.

Things to see and do in Beersheba reflect the city's character as "Capital of the Negev". Catch up on the history of the city and the desert at the **museum,** housed in a disused Turkish mosque (built in 1915) set in its own little park. **Abraham's Well** can still be seen on the Hebron road (Keren Kayemet Street), well worn and probably reconstructed many times over the centuries.

To the Dead Sea

The Jericho road from Jerusalem passes around the Mount of Olives and then through the Arab town of El-Azariye, or **Bethany.** The Arab name comes from Azar, or Lazarus, for his tomb is here, to the left off the road and up the hill. Jesus visited Bethany and called Lazarus forth from the tomb *(John 11: 41–44)*, making this a happy rather than a

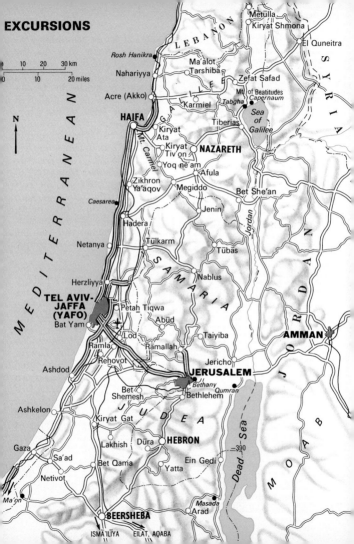

EXCURSIONS

Metulla
Kiryat Shmona
El Quneitra
LEBANON
Rosh Hanikra
Ma'alot
Tarshiha
Nahariyya
Zefat Safad
SYRIA
Acre (Akko)
Mt. of Beatitudes
Capernaum
Karmiel
Tabgha
Sea of Galilee
HAIFA
Kiryat Ata
Tiberias
Kiryat Tiv'on
Yoq ne'am
NAZARETH
Zikhron Ya'aqov
Afula
Caesarea
Megiddo
Bet She'an
Hadera
Jenin
Netanya
Tūlkarm
Tūbās
Herzliyya
Nablus
SAMARIA
TEL AVIV-JAFFA (YAFO)
Petah Tiqwa
Bat Yam
Abūd
Lod
 Taiyiba
AMMAN
Ramla
Rāmallah
Rehovot
Jericho
Ashdod
JERUSALEM
Bethany
Qumran
Bet Shemesh
Bethlehem
Ashkelon
Kiryat Gat
JUDEA
Dead Sea
Gaza
Lakhish
Dūra
HEBRON
Sa'ad
Ein Gedi
–390
MOAB
Netivot
Bet Qama
Yatta
Ma'on
Masada
Arad
BEERSHEBA
ISMA'ILIYA   EILAT, AQABA

MEDITERRANEAN

GALILEE

Mt. Carmel

JORDAN

10   20   30 km
10   20 miles

N

sombre sepulchre. A Crusader fortress-convent and a modern Franciscan church are near the tomb.

As the road descends from Jerusalem to the Jordan River, it passes through wasteland almost completely barren except for a few Bedouin tents. Brace yourself for an astonishing experience when here in the middle of the desert you will suddenly pass a sign marking sea level, as Jericho, the Jordan and the Dead Sea are all well below the level of the Mediterranean.

About 10 kilometres before Jericho, you can take a side trip into the Wadi Qelt gorge. The **Greek Orthodox Monastery of St. George** built into the cliff side once catered to thousands of monks. Today, only a handful live in the isolated monastery, remaining true to the timeless disciplines of simple living and prayer.

Moses first gazed on the Promised Land from a hill opposite **Jericho,** said to be the oldest city in the world, and the first to be conquered by the Israelites led by Joshua *(Josh. 6:1–21).* People still come today wanting to see the famous "walls of Jericho", forgetting that they came tumbling down long ago. A great mound of rubble now marks the spot where the ancient city was built. Nearby, the Mount of Temptation is said to be the place where Jesus was tempted by Satan *(Matt. 4:8–11).*

The highway junction just south of Jericho is where you join the road to **Qumran.** The Dead Sea scrolls (see p. 87)

The Dead Sea

The Dead Sea is spellbinding: it is the lowest place on the face of the earth, 390 metres (1,280 feet) below sea level. Evaporation from the lake takes place faster than the influx of the Jordan's waters, keeping a cloud of haze above the lake and causing the water level to drop slowly. Almost a quarter of the water's volume is mineral matter, making the water undrinkable—almost unsniffable—and giving it a soapy feel. Nothing can live in the waters of the aptly named Dead Sea; but swimming in it will provide you with one of the world's strangest sensations. Try it and see.

The lake is a mineral bonanza, just waiting to be fully exploited. Potash is already manufactured here, and millions of tons of other minerals are there to be reclaimed. Plans have been discussed for a canal to bring water in from the Mediterranean, to provide a solution to the ever-shrinking volume of the Dead Sea.

No hands! In the mineral-saturated Dead Sea, even non-swimmers easily stay afloat.

were discovered in this area, once occupied by a Jewish sect called the Essenes who spent their time farming, studying the holy law and trying to live the moral life. Ruins of their settlement are clearly marked for easy touring.

The road goes through the popular Dead Sea resort of **Ein Gedi,** a good place for lunch, a swim or a walk on the nature trails.

Even farther south along the Dead Sea, you come to **Masada.** As you approach it, you can see that this one flat-topped mountain stands apart from the others, making it perfect for a fortress. It was at Masada that the last group of Jewish Zealots held out in the rebellion against Rome. By A.D. 73 the Romans had held the mountain in siege for three years. Unable to get any more food or water, the Jewish defenders committed mass suicide rather than give the Romans the triumph of capturing them.

An inn, youth hostel, snack bar and kosher restaurant are at the foot of the mountain near the cable car station. If you decide to climb to the 1,450-foot high summit*, be advised that the Snake Path facing the Dead Sea is long and hard (an hour or so for the climb up), but the Bank Path on the western side of the mountain is much easier. Beware of the heat and start your climb early, for it's very hot even in spring and autumn. Even if you choose to take the cable car, drink much more liquid than normal. Dehydration and sunstroke are common afflictions here.

At the top of Masada, cisterns provide drinking water and signs mark the sites of important structures. Even with the well-stocked granaries and reservoirs kept by the defenders here, it still seems miraculous that they could have held out for three years against the vastly superior forces of the Roman legions.

* As a result of the low altitude of the region, the summit is actually only about 135 feet above sea level.

Sea of Galilee

Whether you stop for a swim or not, don't miss a lunch or dinner of fresh lakefish at **Tiberias** (Tveriya), an old and pretty town (now one of Israel's most popular seaside resorts) on the shore of Lake Kinneret, the Sea of Galilee. After the destruction of Jerusalem in A.D. 70, Tiberias became a centre for rabbinic study: the Mishnah (part of the Talmud) was finished here, and the Hebrew alphabet refined; Maimonides, one of Judaism's greatest religious philosophers, is buried in Tiberias, as is Yohanan Ben Zakkai, the 1st-century Rabbi around whom the Jewish people rallied after the destruction of Jerusalem.

At TABGHA, north of Tiberias, is the Church of the

Masada: Zealots in unbelievable privation held off Rome's army.

Multiplication, where Jesus fed the multitudes with only a few loaves and fishes *(Matt. 14:19–20)*. Four kilometres from Tabgha, on the road to Capernaum, a glance at the small Mount of Beatitudes shows why Jesus chose it as the place for the Sermon on the Mount *(Matt. 5, 6, 7):* the small hill is a perfect natural pulpit.

Jesus chose his first disciples from among the fishermen of **Capernaum** (Kefar-Nahum), and the foundations of a house here are said to be those of Simon Peter's. But Capernaum's most important ruins are those of a large and rich **synagogue** in the Roman style, built soon after Jerusalem's destruction. Simon Peter's house and the synagogue are conveniently placed next door to one another.

Also in Galilee, halfway between Tiberias and Haifa, is **Nazareth,** the town where Jesus grew up. Today, the population is almost evenly divided among Jews, Christians and Moslems. The **Church of the Annunciation** is a tremendous modern monument built for the Franciscans in the 1960s. It is constructed over the grotto where Mary received the news that she would bear a son and should call him Jesus *(Luke 1:28–35).*

Haifa and Environs

The third largest city in Israel, **Haifa** is known for both its industry and scenic beauty. It is dominated by the verdant heights of Mount Carmel ("God's Vineyard"), mentioned several times in the Bible for its beauty. After many centuries of colourful history, which included Crusader conquest, the city was destroyed in the 18th century. Its rebirth came in the 19th as European immigrants began to arrive, and started to plan the new Haifa, which Theodor Herzl had predicted would be the "city of the future". The builders' success is evident, as despite the ships, factories and trade centres Haifa is full of parks and beaches, tree-lined streets and sweeping vistas.

Get into the mood of Haifa by taking a ride on the Carmelit, the city's useful underground train which leaves from Paris Square near the Customs House and climbs the heights of **Mount Carmel,** making a number of stops along the way. At the upper terminus are several attractive residential quarters, and also Rehov Yefe Nof, the aptly named "Panorama Road", from which you may scan the whole city and its port. Higher up are to be found

Haifa University and the new Technion whereas just below Panorama Road are the Persian Gardens which surround the Baha'i Shrine, resting-place of Mirza Ali Muhammad, the 19th-century visionary. He was known to his followers as the "Gate of Faith" (Bab ed-Din) through whose leadership they would be able to enter paradise.

Down the slopes of Mount Carmel is the centre of modern Haifa, the business area called Hadar Ha'Carmel. Herzl Street is its lifeline, with shops and various services including a Government Tourist Information Office. The great Turkish palace called the Old Technion which looms above Herzl Street was begun in 1913 with funds donated by German Jews.

EL KARMIL, 22 kilometres south-east of Haifa, will introduce you to the daily life of the Druze people, whose Moslem-inspired religious beliefs are kept a closely-guarded secret. EIN HOD, 12 kilometres south of Haifa, is a small former Arab village, restored by Israeli painters and sculptors to become famous as an artists' colony.

Caesarea, almost exactly half-way between Haifa and Tel Aviv, was built in about 20 B.C. by Herod the Great and named after the emperor Caesar Augustus. The city's history is a gory tale. In A.D. 66 it was the site of a Jewish uprising against the Romans; in 1101 it was taken by the Crusaders; in 1187 by Saladin, and in 1191 by Richard the Lion-Heart, only to be destroyed by Mameluke invaders the following century. Thereafter it was left in peace and ruins until the late 19th century.

With its ancient walls and gates, bridges, towers and fortifications, the **Crusader city** is worth visiting. Other impressive ruins near the city include the large 2nd-century **Roman amphitheatre** (popular for summer concerts and theatre) and **aqueduct.**

Today, the town is essentially a holiday centre amply provided with sandy beaches, sailing boats and sunny days.

North of Haifa is **Acre** (Akko), capital city of the region from Phoenician times until early in the present century. Similar to Caesarea's storybook history, Acre's past included visits by Caesar and Saladin, the Knights of St. John, Richard the Lion-Heart and Napoleon Bonaparte who laid siege to the town in 1799 but eventually had to retreat. You can still see much evidence from this romantic past within **79** the medieval walls of the Old City. The **Mosque of El Jezzar** is the city's most impressive, built in 1781 by the ferocious Turkish governor, Ahmed Jezzar Pasha. Next to the mosque is the **Hammam el-Pasha,** once the mosque's luxurious Turkish bath, now furnished as Acre's museum. The **Citadel's** foundations date from Crusader times, although the construction is mostly Turkish. A look at the "crypt", actually the knights' dining hall, will get you right in the spirit of Crusader days.

The northern coast of Israel abounds in beautiful places to sun and swim, but **Nahariyya** is the spot preferred by those who know them all. A cooling stream ripples along a canal in the middle of the town's main street, and shady café tables along the waterfront provide another sort of respite from the hot summer sun. Nahariyya is crowded on Saturdays, so it is better to plan your visit for a weekday. As a diversion, go by bus (in summer) or by taxi to ROSH HANIKRA, atop the cliffs on the Lebanese border. A cable car will take you down the cliffside to its base so you can explore the grottoes formed and shaped over thousands of years by the constant washing of the waves.

Tel Aviv—Jaffa

Jaffa (Yafo) has been Jerusalem's port since biblical times, but **Tel Aviv** is completely new. It grew haphazardly to fill the needs of the floods of Jewish immigrants arriving during this century, and soon the throbbing modern metropolis engulfed the sleepy Arab town of Jaffa. Now, with big hotels crowding the seafront and high-rise blocks spreading through the city, brash and worldly Tel Aviv is the nerve centre of Israel's commercial, industrial and cultural life. It has little of Jerusalem's fascination and beauty, but life here provides a change of pace from the weighty sanctity of the Holy City.

Start your sightseeing from the **observation platform** on the tall office building called the Shalom Tower off Allenby Street; it's the best place for a general view of the urban sprawl. Next, visit the city's modern **Great Synagogue,** not far from the tower. Habimah National Theatre and Mann Auditorium, a short distance from the centre of the city, are the attractive, modern focal points of Israel's cultural life, home of the nation's repertory theatre company and of the famed Israel Philharmonic Or-

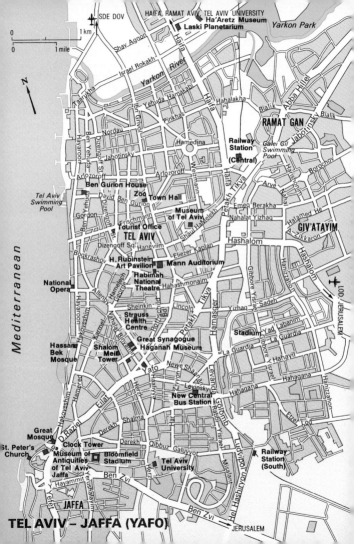

TEL AVIV – JAFFA (YAFO)

chestra. The Helena Rubinstein Art Pavilion is near Habimah on Sderot Tarsat.

As for museums, Tel Aviv has close to two dozen of them, preserving everything from David Ben-Gurion's house to specimens of Bronze Age glass. Several museums are grouped together in the **Ha'Aretz Museum** complex in Ramat-Aviv, the suburb north of the Yarkon River. Among others, the Haganah Museum, 23 Rothschild Boulevard, is one of the more interesting places, with exhibits outlining the military history of the country in this century. The Museum of Tel Aviv, 33 Sderot Shaul

Tel Aviv, big town with a global focus: sprawling, bustling, modern. Some 400,000 people live, work and play in the seaside metropolis.

HaMelekh, has collections of art in various media, and rooms for chamber music concerts. Finally, the **Museum of the Jewish Diaspora** (Beth Hatefutsoth) is a fascinating place. With dioramas and models, photographs and films, the history of the Jewish people from the destruction of the Temple in A.D. 70 to 1948 is recounted.

Tel Aviv explodes with lights, colour and activity on Saturday nights, especially along **Dizengoff Street** between

Visit to a Kibbutz

Israel's collective settlements, called kibbutzim, are world famous. Jewish communal settlements go back to biblical times, but the kibbutz movement was started here in 1909. In the early days, life on a kibbutz was filled with strenuous work and few pleasures but much satisfaction in community life and development. Today the work is still taxing, whether it be factory work or agricultural labour, but life is more comfortable.

You can get a close-up look at these fascinating communes by staying at a Kibbutz Inn. About twenty kibbutzes have inns on their land, rated as three- or four-star hotels, catering to visitors and adding income to the kibbutz's funds. Reservations are made through the central office for Kibbutz Inns in Tel Aviv at 100 Allenby Road, Box 1139, tel.: 615-719 or 614-879.

Helfried Weyer, Nauborn-Wetzlar

Gordon Street and Dizengoff Square. Old people rest on benches by the fountains in the square, but the young prefer the outdoor cafés for sitting and the crowded streets for strolling. Flirting is what Saturday night was made for, and it spices up the already rich potpourri of Dizengoff Street. When the cinemas disgorge their masses, the action gets an **83** extra boost. That's when no one can mistake Tel Aviv for Jerusalem!

Jaffa, on a promontory overlooking the Mediterranean, is much more sedate both by day and night. Fast becoming Tel Aviv's "artists' colony", Jaffa has some of the city's most attractive art galleries, boutiques, cafés and restaurants, most of them located near St. Peter's Catholic Church and Monastery. A walk reveals parks and gardens, an old Ottoman clock tower and mosque, an archaeological dig, and the Museum of Antiquities of Tel Aviv-Yafo. Work of tidying up the town, deserted by its Arab residents after the fighting in 1948, still goes on.

In the Caliph's Court at Baghdad: scene in Tel Aviv's Diaspora Museum.
Right: Shrine of the Book's gleaming dome protects priceless scrolls.

What to Do

Museums

In such a historical city, it's no wonder fine museums abound. They charge very reasonable fees, some nothing at all. See pp. 120–122 for opening hours.

The **Israel Museum** is the country's largest and most inclusive. In the main buildings, the Bronfman Biblical and Archaeological collection traces the thread of Jewish and related art histories through the centuries, with everything from ancient menorahs to Tunisian Jewish wedding costumes. The Bezalel collection focuses on modern painting and sculpture, especially (but not exclusively) relating to Israel. There's also a fine collection of Islamic art.

Nearby, the architecturally exciting **Shrine of the Book** has striking displays of the precious Dead Sea Scrolls (see p. 87). Outside the museum, works by Lipschitz, Maillol, Rodin and

Israel Museum holds 5,000 years of history, a lot for one lesson.

others dot the pebble-strewn walks of the **Billy Rose Art Garden.**

Jerusalem's Islamic Museum, next to El-Aksa Mosque, holds the city's widest-ranging collection of works by Moslem artists who made tiles, carved wood and stone, illuminated manuscripts, calligraphy and intricate inlaid work.

For another collection of Islamic works of art, visit the L.A. Mayer Institute, 2 Rehov HaPalmakh, where antique firearms and swords add drama to domestic items such as glassware and pottery, jewellery and cloths.

Archaeological collections abound in Jerusalem. The best is in the **Rockefeller Museum,**

The Dead Sea Scrolls

In 1947, two Arab shepherd-boys searching for a wayward goat stumbled across a hidden cave in the rocks near Qumran on the shores of the Dead Sea. In the cave were eight large clay jars containing several parchment scrolls and fragments wrapped in ancient linen.

Several weeks later, the boys' uncle sold their find for a few pounds to a merchant in Bethlehem. Later, when the scrolls came into the hands of Hebrew University archaeologists in Jerusalem, researchers slowly began to realize that the discovery was one of the most significant ever to have been made in religious history.

Among other scrolls was a complete script of the Old Testament book of Isaiah, 1,000 years older than any previously know codex. Comparing it with modern translations, experts found that the old and new versions were almost exactly the same—a triumph for many scholars as the discovery lent credence to the authority of the biblical writings and demonstrated that years of painstaking effort to faithfully reproduce the ancient texts had been successful.

The Dead Sea Scrolls have still to yield all their secrets. Far from caves and clay jars, most of the priceless documents are now housed in the "Shrine of the Book" museum in Jerusalem.

which traces man's progress from the area's Iron Age inhabitants through biblical, Greek and Roman times to the flourishing of Islam. You can pay your respects to the bones of Mount Carmel Man, who lived over 100,000 years ago. Smaller archaeological collections are in the Pontifical Bible Institute, Rehov Paul Emil Botta, and at the YMCA not far from the King David Hotel.

The **Old Yishuv Court Museum,** 6 Rehov Or Hayyim, in the Old City's Jewish Quarter, gives a glimpse into the daily life of the "Old Yishuv", the Jewish community living here before the 19th- and 20th-century waves of immigration. This private-home-turned-museum has each room decorated in mid-19th-century Ottoman style, and guest rooms for Ashkenazim (with European furniture) and Sephardim (with oriental sofas and braziers). Period photographs highlight a good collection of artisans' implements, showing how they were used a century or more ago.

Sports

Most sports are available in Israel, but considering the generally hot climate, it's not surprising that water activities of all kinds tend to be the most popular. Diving, water-skiing and sailing facilities can be found at most of Israel's seaside resorts.

Warmest for winter swimming is **Eilat** on the Red Sea. This paradise for divers offers equipment for hire, courses for beginners and glass-bottomed boats for enthusiasts who like to admire the fish and keep dry at the same time. Of the Mediterranean beaches in the south, **Ashkelon** has a very fine strand. Then, **Bat Yam** and **Herzliyya** are just on the outskirts of Tel Aviv with the resorts of **Netanya** and **Caesarea** (see p. 79) a little farther north. In the Haifa area, **Nahariyya** (see p. 80) is one of the best places for a day by the sea.

In Jerusalem itself, the YMCA indoor pool is open all

Sea of Galilee: Jesus once calmed its stormy waters, and Jewish scholars such as Maimonides lived on its shores. Today it's a resort.

year round. Otherwise there are pools at Kyriat Hayovel south of the Mount Herzl area and, farther out, at Ramat Rachel kibbutz above the Bethlehem road and Kfar Hanofesh in the woods near Yad Vashem. The swimming season extends from May to September.

Football (soccer) and basketball are usually well-attended spectator sports and it's often difficult to get tickets. There are stadiums at the Hebrew University of Jerusalem and in Tel Aviv.

Many centres offer tennis and a few, riding facilities; there's an 18-hole golf course at Caesarea.

Ronald Sheridan, Harrow-on-the-Hill

Shopping

Bridging the gap between the West and the Orient, Jerusalem has large and modern department stores as well as eastern bazaars. For the former, try Jaffa Road between Zion Square and Makhane Yehuda. If it's handiwork and craft items you're after, the narrow streets of Old Jerusalem are filled with tiny shops overflowing with olivewood figurines, gold and silver jewellery with precious and semi-precious stones, ceramic pieces, trays, cups, Turkish coffee sets and candelabra of gleaming copper and brass. Leather articles, hand-woven cloths, embroidered dresses and shirts are beautiful and tempting. Many shops carry similar pieces so it's a good idea to shop around.

If you buy inlaid work, be sure the box or backgammon set really has inlay, for some ingenious decal (transfer) manufacturer has come up with films that look very like the real thing—you have got to inspect the piece very closely to detect the difference. At almost any shop in Old Jerusalem you can have your name—in Latin, Hebrew or Arabic letters—cut from a sheet of gold or silver and made into a pendant or clip.

89

Two establishments specializing in high-quality craft items are Khutzot Hayotzer, in a lane of restored old-fashioned shops just south of the Citadel on Jerusalem Brigade Road; and the Jerusalem House of Quality, 12 Hebron Road (buses Nos. 4, 6, 7 or 18).

Shopping hours are usually from 8 a.m. to 1 p.m. and 4 to 7 p.m., though on the eve of the Jewish or Moslem Sabbaths shopkeepers may close around 2 p.m. Some shops have a half-day closing on either Tuesday or Wednesday afternoons. Jewish shops are closed on Saturday, Moslem ones on Friday, Christian ones on Sunday. As a result of Jerusalem's three Sabbaths and variable hours, you'll soon realize that the bazaar is active more or less seven days a week.

Israel has a Value Added Tax of 12 per cent which may be added to your bill or included in the price—ask to be sure which is the case. If you pay in foreign currency, many shops are authorized to waive the V.A.T. Some shops and stores have duty-free schemes whereby you can purchase an item, have it delivered at the dock or airport when you leave for home, and receive a 30 per cent discount on the price. This system is widely applied especially in the case of shops dealing in leather clothing. Be sure to do your sums before you buy, and it's better to make certain that the discounted price is really a bargain over normal prices in other shops—it's not always!

Glittering shop windows delight the eye, but on hot days an ice cool drink is as good as gold.

Nightlife

Though Jerusalem has a few nightclubs and smoke-filled cabarets, its evening entertainments are mostly of a more sedate kind. The open-air **sound and light show** in the Citadel (see p. 122 for times of performance) is well worth while seeing. Dress much more warmly than you think is necessary—everyone underestimates the chill. Tickets are on sale at the Citadel entrance by Jaffa Gate.

On Wednesday evenings, **folkdance performances** are given in the Khan theatre, south of the Montefiore Windmill across the street from the railway station. The Kahn, a refurbished Ottoman caravanserai, also has a restaurant and bar, and is worthy of a look in itself. Get details of current folkdance offerings from one of the Israel Government Tourist Offices.

The larger hotels in West Jerusalem often schedule **folk song evenings** with Israeli performers and perhaps even a jolly audience sing-along. If your hotel has no such evening, consult the daily newspapers or the Tourism Ministry's bulletin, *Events in the Jerusalem Region*, for information on shows.

Jerusalem has a rich cultural life at night. A half-dozen halls and theatres host concerts and recitals, drama and ballet. The city's cinemas are located mainly in West Jerusalem. Films are screened in the original language with Hebrew, English or French subtitles. Cinemas are well-attended (often with somewhat brash and noisy crowds), especially on Saturday evenings, and it's a good idea to buy your tickets a half-hour or so in advance of the screening time. In East Jerusalem the cinemas are usually well-filled also, but films in this part of the city tend to be in Arabic only—entertaining and

Immigrants from many countries have added their costumes, dances and songs to Jerusalem's own. Vibrant performances bring them to life.

romantic, but very mysterious to those who do not understand the language.

For **nightclubs,** make the rounds of West Jerusalem's big hotels to find the ones with the best shows, which tend to be folkloric rather than titillating in this sacred city. In East Jerusalem, Arabic nightclubs and some restaurants offer intriguing but fairly subdued oriental dancing, plus delightful Arabic music.

Young people out for danc-ing to loud rock bands need only stroll around Zion Square and Ben Yehuda Street at 8 or 9 o'clock in the evening, letting their ears lead them to the currently popular club, often a few dim and diminutive rooms on the second floor, weak on decor but strong on good music and good vibrations. For that cosy café table for two, walk along Rivlin Street, south of Jaffa Road near Bar Kokhba Square, and see which of the little cafés will suit your taste.

Dining

Jerusalem's cuisine is as polyglot as its people, and no one but a foreigner would think it strange to find goulash, gefilte fish, *falafel*, snails and hamburgers on the same menu. Settlers from all over the world brought their native cooking with them, adapted it to the produce of the Holy Land, made it kosher, added a dash of Arabic flavour, and ended up with the astonishing and sometimes bewildering mixture of Jerusalem food.

Breakfast

Those used to a slice of toast and a cup of coffee in the morning may be overwhelmed by a Jerusalem breakfast. Both Arab and Israeli-run hotels tend to present mammoth meals, often weighing down a huge buffet table: eggs cooked several ways, fresh fruits and juices, pickled fish and vegetables, different kinds of olives and cheeses, *khumus* (a chickpea puree), purees of vegetables and beans, sliced tomatos, a half-dozen kinds of bread, cakes and rolls, yogurt, and even cornflakes. There is a real danger of overeating and ending up back in bed rather than on the sightseeing trail. If you

enjoy coffee at breakfast, you may find it better to settle for instant rather than the disappointing liquid which is normally served as "fresh-brewed", or switch to tea.

Lunch

The plenitude of breakfast is matched only by the sturdy Jerusalem lunch, usually the main meal of the day, with a meat course. As certain traditional rules relating to food *(kashrut)* require at least six

Purveyors for a dozen cuisines, bazaar shops can please anyone.

hours to pass between the eating of meat and the eating of dairy products, Israelis tend to avoid things such as steak with potatoes topped by butter, or cheeseburgers.

If a heavy lunch is too much for you in the summer heat, many cafés and small restaurants have light luncheon plates of fried eggs and sandwiches.

Keeping Kosher

Judaism's dietary laws are observed more often than not in Israel, and so Jews who keep strictly to kosher meals find no problem. Virtually all of the hotels in West Jerusalem serve only kosher meals in their restaurants as a matter of course, and most other dining-places in this part of the city are kosher as well—even the Chinese, Russian and American places.

You will find it nearly impossible to have milk and meat products together at the same meal, but otherwise dinner in a kosher restaurant is likely to be much the same as you're used to at home.

In East Jerusalem the hotels and restaurants generally are not kosher, though the prohibition of pork familiar to Jews is also a Moslem tenet. Seafood must have fins and scales to be kosher, and so you'll find no shellfish in Jewish restaurants. Moslem chefs tend to go along with this prohibition, though the Koran does not specifically ban shellfish from the diet.

Smoked turkey, which substitutes quite deliciously for the forbidden ham, is a good choice. Pickled vegetables are served at all times and under all circumstances. A big lunch is best followed by an hour's nap.

Dinner

For Jerusalemites, dinner at home is often a salad and cheese or some other light repast, though the city's restaurants are geared to foreign habits and provide full-course dinners. French, Chinese, German, Italian, Hungarian, Russian and American meals are all easy to come by, and in East Jerusalem the Arab restaurants are endless. A favourite Arab meat dish is *shwarma,* rounds of lamb stacked on a vertical spit

and grilled against a vertical charcoal or gas grill, the cooked outer layer of the meat being sliced off and served when done.

Lamb comes in all forms, including such dubious delicacies as fried brains, stuffed heart, or both of these in a mixed grill. Green salad or a "Turkish salad" of chopped vegetables in a very spicy dressing may accompany your meat dish.

Desserts are European or Middle Eastern. Many immi-

Exotic? After a few bites you may learn how to make it at home.

grants came from Central Europe, and Viennese-style coffee-houses abound, complete with *Sachertorte* and *kleine braune.* Flan is frequently found on dessert menus. But to know Jerusalem you must taste its *baklava,* a sweet flaky pastry of ground nuts and honey. *Burma,* a Turkish dessert, is made of shredded wheat rolls **97**

stuffed with whole pistachio nuts and soaked in syrup or honey. *Mohalabíyeh*, an Arab treat, is a bland milk-and-rose-water pudding.

Snacks

If there is a dish to unite Arabs and Israelis, it is *falafel*, spiced balls of chick-pea meal deep-fried, mixed with chopped vegetables and peppers, stuffed in half a round of flat *píta* (Eastern) bread, and topped with a few spoonfuls of *takhína*, a sesame seed butter. From morning till night hungry Jerusalemites stop at stands all over the city and pay the small price for this tasty snack.

Fresh-squeezed fruit and vegetable juices are an important thirst-quencher in the hot months, and juice bars can be found with little trouble, anywhere in the city. Unfortunately, *falafel* stands and juice bars are often some distance from one another, but the *falafel* sandwich is eminently portable.

Beverages

Soft drinks, including some familiar international brands, and a local fizzy mineral water,

Attacking a falafel *sandwich can demand some mighty manœuvrings.*

are on sale everywhere, competing with fresh juices as thirst-quenchers among devout Moslems, who drink no alcohol.

Coffee and tea are served everywhere, but you must be careful when ordering. Arab cafés will serve you very sweet Turkish coffee unless you ask for it *sokar 'aleel* (with just a pinch of sugar). Your coffee may be perfumed with *hehl* (cardamom seed), a delightful addition. You can often get a glass of "Nes" (instant coffee) instead, if you prefer. Cafés with espresso machines may serve you a fairly tasty cup of "capuccino", which in Jerusalem means coffee with whipped cream. Some cafeterias, snack bars and less-discerning restaurants serve a local speciality coffee made by pouring hot water into a glass with coffee grounds, called *botz* ("mud"). *Botz* looks, smells, tastes and goes down like its namesake, and should be avoided at all costs. Remember to specify which kind of coffee you want when you order or you may find yourself confronted with a serving of *botz*.

The bottled beer is mostly American-style lager—try *Maccabee* or *Gold Star*—though some hotels and bars have a local dark beer as well. **99**

A rolling coffee-shop can follow the crowd: have it Turkish-style or just instant, in a glass.

Imported beers are available, but tend to be much more expensive than the local brew.

Israeli wines are quite palatable, many being exported and enjoyed abroad. Red, white and rosé, dry or sweet, all are easy to come by. *Rose of Carmel*, a dry red, and *Ben Ami*, another of the same type, are among the best.

Though alcohol is forbidden to good Moslems, Arabs who are Christians often drink *arak*, aniseed-flavoured brandy, at mealtimes. With water and ice the *arak* turns a milky colour and is mild enough to drink with the meal, or it can be drunk full-strength as a liqueur. *Golden Arak* is one of the preferred brands. Many Israelis end their meals with *Sabra*, Israel's orange-and-chocolate liqueur, but there are quite a few other brandies and liqueurs to choose from as well.

When you dine in East Jerusalem, remember that some Arab restaurants do not serve alcoholic drinks at all, and others serve them normally but not on the Moslem Sabbath (Thursday sunset to Friday sunset) and holidays.

To Help You Order...

Could we have a table? | **Efshár lekabél shulkhán?**

I'd like a/an/some... | **ten li, bevakashá**

beer	**bíra**	olive oil	**shémen záyit**
bread	**lékhem**	pepper	**pilpél**
butter	**khemá**	potatoes	**tapukhéy-adamá**
cheese	**gviná**	rice	**órez**
chips (french fries)	**chips**	rolls	**lakhmaniyót**
coffee	**kafé**	salad	**salát**
fish	**dag**	salt	**mélakh**
fruit	**peyrót**	sandwich	**sándwich**
ice-cream	**glidá**	soup	**marák**
lemon	**lemón**	sugar	**sukár**
lettuce	**khása**	vegetables	**yerakót**
milk	**khaláv**	vinegar	**khómetz**
mustard	**khardál**	water	**máyim**
		wine	**yáyin**

and Read the Menu...

báklava	sweet flaky pastry with nuts	**kréplakh**	dough envelopes with savoury filling
dag malúakh	herring	**lében**	yogurt
éshel	sour milk	**mohalabíyeh**	milk and rose-water pudding
faláfel	spiced fried chick-pea paste	**piláf**	Turkish-style rice
gefilte fisch	chopped stuffed carp	**pilpél memulá**	stuffed peppers
khálva	honey, almond and sesame cake	**píta**	flat bread
		shnítzel	veal or turkey, breaded and fried
khamuzím	pickled vegetables		
khúmus	chick-pea puree		
kavéd of	chicken liver	**shaménet**	sour cream
kebáb	roast lamb or mutton, or ground meat grilled on wood fire	**shashlík**	skewered meat and vegetables
		shwárma	vertical-roast lamb
		tarnegól hódu	turkey
kúsa	marrow (zucchini) squash	**takhína**	sesame seed paste sauce

How to Get There

From the United Kingdom

BY AIR: There are daily scheduled flights from Heathrow to Ben-Gurion airport at Lod, outside Tel Aviv, a journey of some $5\frac{1}{2}$ hours. Fares available are first class, economy and 10- to 30-day excursions. Reductions are available for students, young people and children.

Charter flights and package tours: These operate throughout the year. Bookings for the Christmas and Easter weeks need to be made well in advance. Prices vary according to the season with October to April considered as the "high" season.

It's possible to find a very cheap flight and choose your own accommodation as part of the package deal for a seven-night stay. You can fly from Cardiff, Gatwick, Luton, Birmingham, East Midlands and Manchester. Package holiday flights also go to Eilat on the Red Sea. Your agent will advise you about cancellation insurance.

BY SEA: *Adriatica* lines operate all year round, the others only from June to September. Besides the car ferries from Venice, Naples, Athens or Malta, there are also Mediterranean cruise ships which include Haifa as a port of call on their itinerary. You can also get to Israel in a couple of weeks cruising from Southampton.

From North America

BY AIR: Jerusalem is linked (via Ben-Gurion Airport) with Boston, Chicago and New York by daily non-stop service. There are also direct flights several times a week from Montreal and Washington, D.C. Many other U.S. and Canadian cities have easy connections through these main points.

The budget fare varies according to season and may be used to purchase a one-way ticket only. Seats may be booked at any time, but must be confirmed seven days before departure. No cancellation fee is imposed if you are unable to go.

The APEX (Advance Purchase Excursion) fare must be booked and paid for 21 days prior to departure and is valid for a period of 6 to 60 days. This fare is subject to a 10% cancellation fee.

The non-affinity group fare must be booked and paid for no later than seven days before departure. A European stop-over is permitted (at additional cost) on the return journey. Cancellation can be made up to five days prior to departure; after that limit there's a 10% penalty.

Youth fares (for travellers between 12 and 24) are valid for a period of 6 to 120 days and are confirmed at the time of booking—as late as five days before departure. The ticket can be extended for an additional fee.

Charter Flights and Package Tours: The most popular Group-Inclusive Tours (GIT) to Israel last from 9 to 14 days, with three- or four-night extensions to Amsterdam, Athens, London or Rome. They include transport, accommodation, breakfast, transfers, sightseeing and all taxes.

Advance Booking Charters (ABC)—for visitors to Israel who wish to spend up to four months touring on their own—offer the flight only, between North American cities and Tel Aviv.

Another excellent travel possibility during low season is the One-Stop Inclusive Tour Charter (OTC) with flight and accommodation.

When to Go

Spring and autumn are ideal times for a visit to Jerusalem. There should be virtually no rain then with comfortably moderate temperatures. Remember that Jerusalem is up in the Judean hills and is usually cooler than other parts of the country. In winter it gets chilly in Jerusalem and rains frequently. On rare occasions it may even snow. Summer heat is intense, though dry. Sunstroke and dehydration are real dangers everywhere in Israel during the summer.

The following chart gives average monthly temperatures in Jerusalem.

	J	F	M	A	M	J	J	A	S	O	N	D
°C	8	10	12	16	20	22	24	25	23	21	16	11
°F	46	50	54	61	68	72	75	75	73	70	61	52

Planning Your Budget

Over the last decades in Israel inflation has always been high and in recent years has reached epic proportions, rising to well over 100% per annum. This makes budget planning a tricky business. A list of local prices given in autumn will almost certainly be higher at Christmas. And, if you had taken your holiday 6 months earlier, things would have been cheaper then.

Israeli citizens are compensated for price rises by receiving salary readjustments several times a year (although the readjustments are not exactly the same as the inflation rate). Prices are usually increased in waves, each wave followed by a period of relative stability. Some prices, e.g. transport, certain food items, public entertainment are controlled and cannot be changed without Government approval.

But, despite the apparent differences of prices when quoted in figures, in practice the tourist is relatively unaffected by inflation, because strong currencies e.g. dollars, sterling, Swiss francs and deutsche marks constantly rise against the shekel. This unit of currency was officially introduced in 1980, replacing the old Israeli pound *(lira)*.

One problem for the tourist is that it's difficult to know how much things ought to cost. But while prices fluctuate, relative values of goods remain fairly constant. Use them as a rule of thumb to help you decide whether you're getting value for money. For instance, petrol (gas) is expensive, but public transport relatively cheap. Fruit and vegetables are fairly cheap, but meat is very expensive. Concerts, cinemas are quite cheap, etc.

In case of inflation changes (if you're likely to be staying in Israel for several months), keep your funds in traveller's cheques or foreign currency, changing only as much as you need.

BLUEPRINT for a Perfect Trip

An A-Z Summary of Practical Information and Facts

Contents

A

AIRPORTS. Ben Gurion (Lod) airport, about 20 kilometres (12 miles) from Tel Aviv, 60 kilometres (37 miles) from Jerusalem, serves the whole country, although some charter flights from Europe go directly to Eilat. The airport is well designed and offers all services including a tourist information and accommodation desk, a nursery, a post office, restaurants, currency-exchange offices and duty-free shops.

Transport: Taxis, buses and *sheruts* (mostly eight-seat Mercedes operating as shared taxis) wait just outside the terminal. You can take your baggage cart right through customs and out to the street.

The best way of getting to Jerusalem is by *sherut*, a 40- to 50-minute trip. *Sheruts* leave as soon as they're full, and operate continuously, day and night. Taxis, a bit faster, are notably more expensive. Taxis and *sheruts* will take you to your hotel in Jerusalem at no extra cost; though some drivers may dispute this, it is the law. The bus to Jerusalem leaves about every 1½ hours between 7.30 a.m. and 5.30 p.m., though there is no service on Sabbaths (Friday from an hour before sunset until Saturday at sunset) and on holidays. The trip by bus takes an hour, and costs one third of the price of a *sherut*.

Departure: Tourists are reminded to reconfirm their reservations 72 hours in advance of scheduled departure. When returning to Ben Gurion airport, ask your hotel to reserve a seat in a *sherut* for you, leaving *at least three hours* before your flight time. The *sherut* will pick you up at your hotel—even in the middle of the night—and get you to the airport in time for the thorough, but courteous, security checks. If you want a bus, they leave from Jerusalem's Central Bus Station at regular intervals between 6.30 a.m. and 6 p.m., Sabbaths excepted. A private shuttle bus service also operates between Ben Gurion airport and hotels and pick-up areas in Jerusalem.

A departure tax is levied on every passenger at the check-in desk. Do not have film in your camera at the airport (see PHOTOGRAPHY).

Domestic flights: Jerusalem has its own tiny airport, Atarot, although *sherut* service from Ben Gurion airport is so handy that hardly anyone uses it. Arkia (Israel Inland Airlines, Ltd.) operates flights between

principal points within Israel, using both Ben Gurion airport and the
smaller Sde Dov airport at Tel Aviv.

Addresses:

El Al: 12 Hillel Street, Jerusalem; tel.: (02) 233333.

Arkia: 19 Jaffa (Yafo) Road, Jerusalem; tel.: (02) 225888/234855.

CAMPING. Camping is highly developed in Israel, and you can reach
sites by car, caravan (trailer), or even by bus. In Jerusalem, there are
shops where you can hire all the necessary camping equipment, from
clothing to tables and seats. Tents and cabins are also for hire on the
sites themselves, and other facilities such as restaurants or shops,
open-air fireplaces, picnic tables, electricity and toilets are always
available. Contact the Israeli Camping Union:

P.O. Box 53, Nahariyya (north of Haifa); tel.: (04) 923366/925392.

CAR HIRE. See also DRIVING. Local companies compete with the
internationally known car hire firms, but it's best to reserve your car a
day or more in advance, no matter which company you choose.

You must be 21 years of age and have held a driving licence for at
least one year. Rates include public liability insurance, property dam-
age, fire and theft, but not the deductable portion of collision coverage,
for which you may choose to pay a small extra charge. Personal injury
coverage for the driver is not included. If you pay by credit card, you
do not have to give a deposit equal to the estimated rental charge. (If
you pay by card or in foreign currency, you are exempt from the 12%
V.A.T. added to the total invoice.)

Often car hire companies feature special arrangements with a certain
number of days' rental and unlimited mileage for a fixed price. Drive
a hired car only on asphalted roads—insurance coverage does not apply
if you drive on back roads or tracks.

CHILDREN. Children are the future of Israel, and in a country of only
$3\frac{1}{2}$ million people which favours population increase, they are a
blessing. Yours will be accepted happily, and your hotel staff will be
glad to arrange for a baby-sitter at night.

Particularly recommended for children in Jerusalem is the **Biblical
Zoo**—the collection includes most of the animals mentioned in the
Bible. The Zoo is located in the north-western district of Romema (bus
No. 8 or 15).

C   The **Natural History Museum** in Mohilever Street in the Emek Refaim district has lots of working models which children favour, as well as displays of animals and birds from all over Israel (bus No. 4, 14 or 18).

For young children, the **Islamic Art Museum** at 2 HaPalmakh Street offers interesting exhibits, among them a collection of automats and clocks (bus No. 15).

The **Jerusalem Theatre,** the **Israel Museum** and the **International Cultural Centre for Youth** have programmes, films and spectacles for children and young people. The Youth Centre puts on folklore and folkdancing shows every Saturday evening.

Finally it's worth seeking out the **playground** in the distant Kyriat HaYovel quarter (on the way to Hadassah Hospital), for it has the world's most fearsome children's slide. The gigantic black-and-white spike-headed monster has three scarlet tongues down which neighbourhood children glide giggling to the bottom (bus No. 20).

For hours, see SIGHTSEEING HOURS.

CIGARETTES, CIGARS, TOBACCO. Jerusalem's tobacco shops sell most internationally known brands of cigarettes, plus a selection of imported cigars and a dozen different kinds of pipe tobacco (mostly Dutch). Imported cigarettes cost twice as much as local brands.

Time is the most popular medium-strength filter cigarette, and is to Israelis what *Alia* or *Welcome* is to Arabs. For a stronger cigarette try *Nelson* or *Broadway* (Israeli), and *Imperial* or *Omar* (Arab). For a mentholated smoke, buy *Montana. Europa*, exceedingly mild, is sometimes called "the cigarette for people who don't smoke".

The Sabbath is a "non-smoking day" in many restaurants.

CLOTHING. Dress is informal in Israel, as the heat makes jacket-and-tie formality impossible. But religious decorum demands that women have shoulders and heads covered in mosques and synagogues. Short skirts and shorts or slacks on women are not acceptable in holy places (for men cardboard skull-caps are usually provided, but you may find it convenient to buy an inexpensive nylon one to keep with you).

In summer's intense heat, breezy cotton clothing is best, with a light pullover for the evening cool. A broad-brimmed hat and sunglasses are absolutely essential. In winter, Jerusalem can be wet and chilly; bring a light raincoat in January and make sure to have a comfortable pair of

108   shoes (sandals in summer).

Post offices in Israel handle letters and parcels, and also telephone, telegraph and telex operations. Most Jerusalem letter boxes are red English-style pillar boxes. Others are white and blue and bear the postal symbol of a leaping deer. Shops and kiosks which sell stamps, and newspaper shops which have a post office agency, carry the same sign.

Hours (Central Post Office):

Sunday to Thursday: 8 a.m. to 6 p.m.
Friday: 8 a.m. to 2 p.m.
Closed on Saturdays and holidays.

Poste restante (general delivery): If you don't know ahead of time where you'll be staying, you can have your mail sent poste restante to whichever town is most convenient. In Jerusalem, use the Central Post Office (see below).

It can take around $1^{1}/_{2}$ weeks for a letter to reach you from Europe or North America. Have your passport with you for identification.

Telegrams and Telex: Telegrams can be sent 24 hours a day from the Telegraph Office in Jerusalem's Central Post Office. Telex offices, in the same building, are open during normal post office hours. If the party you're contacting has a telex machine, send your message this way—it's much cheaper than by telegraph. You can find their telex number in directories at the office.

Telephone: Israel's telephone system is managed by the Post Office, and though it is very modern, lines are often insufficient to carry the large number of calls. Patience, on the phone, is a virtue. You can dial a call to any part of the country from a public telephone, using the necessary city prefix. You'll need telephone tokens, *asimonim,* for most public phones. They're on sale at some newspaper kiosks and in post offices but they're difficult to find easily if you need one and are in a hurry. Do not insert more than three tokens at a time, as they tend to get stuck, but watch out that there is at least one spare all the time. Using a public telephone is cheaper than calling from a hotel or a shop. For expensive international calls, have the operator in the post office make it for you.

Jerusalem's telephone directories are published in both Hebrew and English.

Jerusalem's Central Post Office: 23 Jaffa (Yafo) Road.

East Jerusalem: Salahedin Street, opposite Herod's Gate.

C **COMPLAINTS.** Jerusalem's hotels, restaurants and shops are so used to welcoming foreign visitors that complaints are usually handled satisfactorily on the spot. If you have to appeal to a higher authority, the Israel Government Tourist Office and the Municipal Tourist Information Office (see TOURIST INFORMATION OFFICES) stand ready to help. Government Tourist Offices have a special form to register complaints.

CONSULATES and EMBASSIES. Jerusalem is Israel's capital city, though some foreign nations still maintain their embassies in Tel Aviv. Because Jerusalem was once divided, some nations have consulates in both parts of the city.

Office hours are generally from 9 a.m. to 12 noon, but some will answer between 4 and 6 p.m.

Australia, Embassy: 185 Hayarkon Street, Tel Aviv; tel.: (03) 243152.

Canada, Embassy: 220 Hayarkon Street, Tel Aviv; tel.: (03) 228122.

Great Britain*, Consulate-General: Tower House (near Railway Station), Jerusalem; tel.: (02) 637619/637724.
Consulate: Sheikh Jarrah, Jerusalem; tel.: (02) 282481/82.
Embassy: 192 Hayarkon Street, Tel Aviv; tel.: (03) 249171.

South Africa, Embassy: 2 Kaplan Street, Tel Aviv; tel.: (03) 256147.

U.S.A., Consulate-General: 18 Gershon Agron Street, Jerusalem; tel.: (02) 223491/225267/68/69.
Consulate: Nablus Road, Jerusalem; tel.: (02) 282231/272681/82.
Embassy: 71 Hayarkon Street, Tel Aviv; tel.: (03) 54338.

CONVERTER CHARTS. For fluid and distance measures, see page 112. Israel uses the metric system.

Length

* Also for citizens of Eire.

Weight

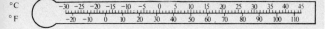

Temperature

CRIME. In general, Jerusalem must be one of the safest cities in the world, though pickpockets are a real menace in crowded buses and in the narrow streets of the bazaar. Wallets, handbags, even rings and wrist-watches can disappear in the throng.

DRIVING IN ISRAEL

To take your car into Israel you will need:

- a valid driving licence (see below)
- car registration papers
- an insurance certificate

You must have either an International Driving Licence or a national driving licence issued by a country which recognizes the Israeli licence. (If your national licence is in a language other than English or French, you must get a Hebrew translation or confirmation of it.)

Driving conditions: There is a high rate of accidents and drivers take big risks, so watch out for everything: overloaded trucks, drivers who turn right but put out a left blinker, vehicles without lights, etc. Driving is especially dangerous after the first rains, as all the dirt and grease accumulated during the dry season form a slippery layer on streets; at the same time, drains get blocked and the roads become rivers.

Roads: Except for the excellent motorway (expressway) between Tel Aviv and Jerusalem and the coastal highway from Ashdod to Acre, Israel's roads are normal two-lane ones. They're well maintained, but not built for high-speed driving.

Parking: To park in Jerusalem's streets, which have no parking meters, unless you're very lucky, you'll need a parking card (sold at the entrance of large parking lots and by lottery-ticket or newspaper vendors). Tear

D   off the three tabs on the card which indicate the month, date and hour you park, and display the card in the window.

Traffic Police, see POLICE.

Fuel and Oil. Service stations are not difficult to find in the modern sections of East and West Jerusalem, and towns along the country's highways usually have at least one station. If stations in West Jerusalem are closed because of a Sabbath or holiday, drive to the East, where stations are liable to be open (or vice versa).

Fluid measures

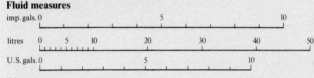

Automobile Club: For help in getting an International Driving Licence or other motoring matters, contact the Automobile Club and Touring Association of Israel (M.E.M.S.I.):

33 Jaffa (Yafo) Road (Beit Yoel building), tel.: (02) 222421.

Breakdowns: A breakdown in the merciless heat of summer can be unpleasant, but although Israel's roads are not heavily travelled, it probably won't take long to get a ride with a passing motorist, or police patrol. If you're driving a hired car, contact the rental agency before having repairs made, except for minor ones such as a flat tire.

DRUGS. The use of drugs is considered a serious problem in Israel, especially among young people. Smoking hashish means immediate eviction from kibbutzes and other places where young visitors may go, and very often, if the case is referred to the police, eviction from Israel. The buying and possession of drugs, if discovered, could entail prison sentences.

E   **ELECTRIC CURRENT.** Israel's current is 220-volt, 50-cycle, as in Europe. Sockets generally take two- or three-pronged European plugs. Transformers and plug adaptors are on sale in most Jerusalem electrical shops.

EMERGENCIES. The police emergency number in Jerusalem, Tel Aviv and Haifa is 100. Depending on the nature of the emergency, see the separate entries in this section such as MEDICAL CARE, CONSULATES, etc.

ENTRY FORMALITIES and CUSTOMS CONTROLS. You will need a valid passport to enter Israel. If you plan to visit an Arab country later, ask the immigration official to put the visa stamp on an immigration form rather than in your passport; most Middle-Eastern countries do not accept passports bearing Israeli stamps. Your entry stamp is good for a stay of three months.

Don't lose the visitor's card that you fill out when entering the country; you may have to show it in the event of a security check or when changing money. It must be handed back at customs upon departure.

Ben Gurion airport uses the "Red" and "Green" channel customs procedure, and tourists with the following items may pass right through the "Green" channel (figures for passengers on return home are given afterwards):

Into:	Cigarettes		Cigars		Tobacco	Spirits		Wine
Israel	250	or	250 g.	or	250 g.	1 l.	and	2 l.
Australia	200	or	250 g.	or	250 g.	1 l.	or	1 l.
Canada	200	and	50	and	900 g.	1.1 l.	or	1.1 l.
Eire	200	or	50	or	250 g.	1 l.	and	2 l.
N. Zealand	200	or	50	or	½ lb.	1 qt.	and	1 qt.
S. Africa	400	and	50	and	250 g.	1 l.	and	1 l.
U.K.	200	or	50	or	250 g.	1 l.	and	2 l.
U.S.A.	200	and	100	and	*	1 l.	or	1 l.
* a reasonable quantity								

When carrying cameras and cine-cameras (one of each plus 10 rolls or reels of film), portable radios and similar items, use the "Red" channel even though these goods are supposed to be duty-free.

When you leave Israel, you will be asked to check your luggage thoroughly to make certain no one has put anything in it without your **113**

E knowledge. There's also a good chance that an official will spot-check your bags.

Currency restrictions: You can bring any amount of local and foreign currency into Israel, and take out local currency up to IS 500, foreign currencies up to the amount imported. You may reconvert up to $3,000 worth of Israeli money to foreign currency; above this limit, you must show currency-exchange receipts proving that you had converted foreign currency in excess of this latter amount upon arrival or during your stay.

G **GUIDES and INTERPRETERS.** You can hire a guide or interpreter by contacting Eshkolot Tours Jerusalem Ltd. (see below). A one-day tour of the city in a private car can easily be arranged. Official guides wear a circular badge, and one may approach you as you enter a tourist area. Be sure to settle the fee in advance. Some taxi drivers are licensed guides. If you see the tourist office symbol of two men bearing a huge bunch of grapes suspended from a pole on the taxi door, chances are that the driver is a licensed guide.

Eshkolot Tours: 36 Keren Hayesod Street, Jerusalem; tel.: (02) 635555/665555.

H **HAIRDRESSERS'.** There are plenty of barbers' shops, hairdressers' and beauty salons throughout the country, but an advance appointment is usually advisable. Prices vary greatly, and a humble local barber may charge only a fraction of what customers at a large hotel's shop must pay.

HITCH-HIKING. Hitch-hiking is done all over Israel, and though on many roads traffic is often light, there is usually little difficulty in getting a ride. Many soldiers and other Israelis wait near bus stops on the highways, hoping for a lift. If no one stops, they can still climb aboard a bus.

HOTELS, HOSPICES, KIBBUTZES and YOUTH HOSTELS. The accommodation desk at Ben Gurion airport can help you find a hotel room if you've arrived without a reservation.

Israel Government Tourist Offices distribute a free guide to the country's hotels published by the Israel Hotel Association. Prices for
hotels are quoted in U.S. dollars, and if you pay in dollars or other

acceptable foreign currency, you are not subject to the 12% Value Added Tax. The room price includes breakfast, usually a substantial one. Children stay at reduced rates: 50% reduction up to the age of six, 30% off for those between six and 12. Air-conditioned rooms are no extra. The service charge, added to all bills, is 15%.

West Jerusalem has the newest and largest hotels, all with kosher restaurants. East Jerusalem has several large hotels, some charming older ones, and a good selection of moderately priced establishments. Rates are constantly rising due to inflation; they're also seasonal, being higher in spring and summer.

Hospices: Various Christian denominations have for centuries provided inexpensive places for pilgrims to stay. You do not have to subscribe to any particular belief to stay in a hospice. Rooms and facilities vary greatly, from plain dormitories to comfortable rooms with bath. Meals are often available as well. Tourist offices in Israel and abroad have lists of hospices, or you can write to the Israel Pilgrimage Committee or the Christian Information Centre (see below).

Kibbutzes: A number of kibbutzes have comfortable three- and four-star hotels on their grounds, operated by kibbutz members. Details of the inns are published in the hotel directory, *Israel Tourist Hotels.*

Youth hostels: Israel has around 30 spare but comfortable youth hostels, a third of them in or near Jerusalem. Hostels are open to everyone regardless of age, marital status, occupation or religion. Visitors with International or Israeli Youth Hostel Cards pay lower rates for bed and board, but even without a card the rates are rock-bottom.

Addresses:

Israel Pilgrimage Committee, 24 King George Street (Government Tourist Information Building), Jerusalem; tel.: (02) 241061.

Christian Information Centre, Omar Ibn el-Khattab Square, Jerusalem; tel.: (02) 287647.

Kibbutz Inns, 100 Allenby Road, Tel Aviv; tel.: (03) 614879.

Israel Youth Hostel Association, 3 Dorot Rishonim Street, Jerusalem; tel.: (02) 222073/225925.

LANGUAGE. The official languages of Israel are Hebrew (by far the most widely spoken) and Arabic. English is spoken or at least understood by most of the people tourists deal with. Because many Israelis were born and raised in other countries, Jerusalem's streets and parlours echo with a symphony—or cacophony—of languages including German, French, the Slavic languages and Spanish.

L   Transcription from Hebrew and Arabic characters to Latin ones adds a further dimension of confusion, and you may see as many as four different spellings of one Hebrew or Arabic word. Place names are another problem. Gates in the city walls, streets, holy sites, and even towns may have a different name in each language: Jerusalem, Yerushalayim, El Kuds. But, though it sounds at first like the Tower of Babel, you should have little problem getting around in the city.

The Hebrew alphabet is used for biblical Hebrew, modern Hebrew and Yiddish. The attractive flow of Arabic script is easy on the eyes but hard on the mind, as Arabic letters may have four different shapes depending on whether the character comes at the beginning, middle or end of a word or is used by itself. In both Hebrew and Arabic, only the consonants are written in most cases.

LAUNDRY and DRY-CLEANING. In the busy summer months it may take three or four days to have clothing dry-cleaned, at other times only two days. Same-day service is available at an extra charge.

All hotels can arrange for your laundry and dry-cleaning to be done. The large ones have their own laundries. In medium-size and smaller hotels, try striking a bargain directly with the chamber-maid as this sometimes results in very fast and very inexpensive service. Lightweight garments washed and hung up in the heat of an Israeli summer will dry in about an hour.

M   **MAPS.** Government Tourist Offices outside Israel are the best source of free maps. The offices in Jerusalem are sometimes undersupplied with the good pictorial, multicoloured map of the city published by the Ministry of Tourism. Car hire firms will provide you with simplified city and country maps when you rent a car, but a better highway map is published by Bank Hapoalim and given away at Government Tourist Offices and branches of the bank.

MEDICAL CARE. If your home insurance cannot be extended to foreign countries, you may want to take out special travel insurance to cover yourself in case of accident, illness or hospitalization during your trip.

By far the most prevalent malady among tourists in Israel is overexposure to sun and heat. You must *not* ignore the sun. Take sunbathing in short half-hour periods at first, and use lotion or sun cream lavishly in summer. No less dangerous is the threat of dehydration, as you lose surprising quantities of body moisture to the dry air without even noticing it. Drink water and other beverages at every opportunity in the hot months, even if you don't feel particularly thirsty. Sunstroke and heat exhaustion are serious ailments—even potentially fatal—though they are easily avoided by tourists who monitor the amount of sun and fluid loss to which they are subjected. Wear sunglasses and a broad-brimmed hat, and tan your feet slowly before wearing sandals all day.

Beware of flies in the Judean desert; one kind causes serious poisoning. It does not occur frequently, but it is well to remember to mention having been in the area if something like a wound that fails to heal appears.

It's best to inquire also, when going to the Red Sea, about poisonous fish and crustaceans—they can be beautiful, but dangerous.

For emergency medical and dental care in Jerusalem, Tel Aviv and Haifa, call the first-aid service of Magen David Adom, the "Red Shield of David", equivalent to the Red Cross. Outside of normal operating hours (see below), they will put you in touch with a doctor or dentist.

The *Jerusalem Post* carries listings of pharmacies and hospital clinics which take turns staying open all night.

Magen David Adom First Aid Centre in Jerusalem is in Romema near the Central Bus Station; open on Fridays and on the eves of holidays from 9 to 12 p.m., and Saturdays and holidays from 10 a.m. to 2 p.m. and 3 to 6 p.m. Bus No. 5, 6 or 7.

Emergency medical and dental telephone number: 101.

MEETING PEOPLE. Though they may squabble among themselves, Jerusalemites have a ready welcome for foreign tourists no matter what their nationality or religion. The greeting you get may be somewhat more sober and dignified than ebullient and smiling, but this is typical of the spirit of the Holy City, and may also have something to do with the complex and preocccupying problems its citizens face daily. *Shalom* (peace) is the word that begins and ends every conversation in West Jerusalem, with *shabbat shalom* taking its place on the Jewish Sabbath. In East Jerusalem, say *salaam aleikum* (peace with you); answer: *aleikum salaam* (with you, peace) or *meh eh salameh* (with peace), or use the simpler *marhaba*—"(God) make your road even" (greeting when meeting someone on his way). In an Arab restaurant you can delight new-found friends with the toast *meh-heh-beh!* (with love!), while in a West Jerusalem restaurant the words are *lekhayim!* (to life!) and *bteh-avon (bon appétit)*.

Remember when making new friends that different cultures follow different ground rules, and there can sometimes be misunderstandings. Best to proceed slowly until each person has some idea of the other's expectations.

M MONEY MATTERS

Currency. The Israel unit of currency is the shekel (abbreviated IS). It is divided into 100 new agorot. Coins in circulation are 1 agora, 5 agorot, 10 agorot and half a shekel (50 agorot). Banknotes are 1 shekel, 5 shekels, 10 shekels, 50 shekels and 100 shekels. Old lirot banknotes and coins are being phased out but are still in circulation. Check your change carefully as the new and old are very similar in appearance but different in value.

Banking hours:

Sunday, Monday, Tuesday and Thursday: 8.30 a.m. to 12.30 p.m. and 4 to 5 or 5.30 p.m.

Wednesday: 8.30 a.m. to 12.30 p.m.

Fridays and the eves of holidays: 8.30 a.m. to 12 noon.

Closed on Saturdays and Jewish religious and national holidays.

In West Jerusalem hotels, subsidiary bank offices have longer hours. In East Jerusalem, money-changers' offices are open during daylight hours, with some offices closing on Fridays, others on Sundays. The currency-exchange desks at Ben Gurion airport are always open.

Changing money: Banks give the best rate of exchange, though your hotel will be glad to change currency for you, as well. Hotels, tour agencies, car hire firms and many other businesses will quote their prices in U.S. dollars as well as shekels. If you pay in dollars (the most convenient currency) or other hard foreign monies, you are exempted from paying the 12% Value Added Tax. Always take your passport with you when changing money.

Credit Cards and Traveller's Cheques: Internationally recognized credit cards and traveller's cheques are accepted by car hire agencies, and the better hotels and restaurants. Paying this way (or with foreign currency) exempts you from Israel's 12% V.A.T. If you pay by traveller's cheque, you may get change in shekels. Take your passport for identification.

N NEWSPAPERS and MAGAZINES.

Besides daily papers in Hebrew and Arabic you will find the *Jerusalem Post* on news-stands every day except Saturday; Friday's edition of the *Post* has a special magazine supplement with feature articles, a calendar of events and a guide to entertainment. The *International Herald Tribune* tends to reach Jerusalem the day following publication, and is sold in hotels and at street-side newspaper stands. Other papers and magazines distributed internationally are also easy to find.

PHOTOGRAPHY. Shops that specialize in photography (not only the sale of film) will readily give you hints on what to do and what to use in Jerusalem. Note that the light in this region with its ultra-violet rays tends to bring out the purple too much, so use, if possible, a UV filter. The best time for photography is 8 a.m. to noon, and at sunset.

Photography is a sensitive subject in Jerusalem, and not just because of the clear and brilliant Israeli sun; taking photographs is not allowed at or near some holy sites—at the Western Wall on the Sabbath, or in the Jewish Orthodox quarter of Mea She'arim for instance. Orthodox Jews and Moslems make fascinating subjects for photographs, but you must never take pictures without asking first, even if you shoot from a distance. Anything having to do with military security is off limits to photographers, including airports and docks.

Tourists leaving Israel at Ben Gurion airport are advised to see to it that their cameras are empty of film when coming to the airport, to facilitate the checking of the camera. Should there be film in the camera, the passenger will be asked to leave it with the airport authorities who will place it in a sealed box which will be carried on the flight on which the passenger is travelling. The camera will then be returned to the passenger at his or her destination.

POLICE. Israel has a national police force to maintain law and order in all cities, towns and the countryside. The force includes Jordanian Arabs who held police positions in East Jerusalem before the 1967 war. Uniforms are khaki in summer and dark blue in winter. Most officers speak some English and are glad to help with any problems.

At traffic intersections, obey the pedestrian signals. Pairs of policewomen patrol the streets in West Jerusalem's central district and fine on the spot those who cross streets contrary to the signals.

In emergencies, dial 100 to reach Jerusalem's Police Headquarters, on Heshin Street, off Jaffa (Yafo) Road in the Russian Compound.

PUBLIC HOLIDAYS and SABBATHS. Jerusalem is a calendar-printer's nightmare, for each religious sect uses its own system of years and dates, and it is no exaggeration to say that if you observed them all, you'd celebrate New Year's Day at least a half-dozen times in one year. Most of these holidays cannot be matched up with the normal (Gregorian) calendar because they are figured in lunar months, or are moveable feasts. The best you can do is keep an eye on local newspapers and events listings. During celebrations of several days, shops and offices run by observers of the holiday may be closed on the first and last

P days of the festivities, and perhaps open for shorter hours the rest of the time.

The Jewish Sabbath (*shabbat*), starting at sunset Friday and lasting until sunset on Saturday, is more strictly observed than is the day of rest in most other countries. All Jewish shops and businesses close, most public transport ceases, and the country is brought nearly to a standstill. In Orthodox quarters, driving of cars and anything else which can be looked upon as work is banned.

Moslems' holy day starts on Thursday at sunset and continues until sunset on Friday; Christians observe the day of rest all day on Sunday.

R **RADIO and TV.** Israel has six radio programmes, broadcast on AM (medium wave), FM and short wave frequencies. News in English is given six times a day. Jordan Radio, from nearby Amman, also features some programmes and news bulletins in English. The Voice of America and BBC Overseas Service can be heard on the AM band when conditions are good.

Both Israeli and Jordanian televisions broadcast in English, Hebrew and Arabic.

The *Jerusalem Post Magazine*, included with the Friday edition of the newspaper, has full radio and television listings for the week to come.

RELIGIOUS SERVICES. Going to a service in Jerusalem has special significance for every visitor. Government Tourist Offices can give you a booklet which lists synagogues and churches with their addresses and service times; it's worth confirming the latter to avoid any disappointment. The Christian Information Centre at Jaffa Gate has most comprehensive lists of Christian holy places and services.

S **SIESTA.** The mid-afternoon snooze is well established in Jerusalem's daily life, and most shops and offices close for at least two hours between 12.30 or 1 p.m. and about 4 p.m. As the midday meal is customarily the largest one of the day, a rest afterwards during the hottest hours is both sensible and healthful.

SIGHTSEEING HOURS

Basilica of the Agony: 8.30 a.m. to 12 noon and 3 p.m. to sunset from April to October, 8.30 a.m. to 12 noon and 2 p.m. to sunset from November to March.

Biblical Zoo: Summer: 8 a.m. to 6 p.m. Winter: 8 a.m. to 4 p.m.
120 Tickets for Saturday must be bought in advance.

Cathedral and Convent of St. James: 3 to 3.30 p.m. on weekdays, 2.30 to 3 p.m. on Saturdays and Sundays.

Church of Mary Magdalene: 9 a.m. to 12 noon, Tuesdays and Saturdays only.

Church and Seminary of St. Anne: 8 a.m. to 12 noon and 2 to 5 p.m. in winter, 2.30 to 6 p.m. only in summer.

Citadel of David: 8.30 a.m. to 4 p.m. in winter, till 5 p.m. in summer.

Dormition Abbey: every day except between 1 and 3 p.m.

Garden Tomb: 8 a.m. to 12 noon and 2 to 5 p.m. daily.

Islamic Museum: 8 a.m. to 5.30 p.m. in summer, to 4 p.m. in winter, closed on Fridays.

Israel Museum: 10 a.m. to 5 p.m. on Sundays, Mondays, Wednesdays and Thursdays; 4 to 10 p.m. on Tuesdays; 10 a.m. to 2 p.m. on Fridays and Saturdays.

Jerusalem Municipal Museum (in Citadel): 8.30 a.m. to 6.30 p.m. daily.

Knesset: 8.30 a.m. to 2.30 p.m. on Sundays and Thursdays except during public holiday periods.

L.A. Mayer Memorial Institute for Islamic Art: 10 a.m. to 12.30 p.m. and 3.30 to 6 p.m. on Sundays, Mondays, Tuesdays and Thursdays; 3.30 to 9 p.m. on Wednesdays; Saturdays from 10.30 a.m. to 1 p.m.; closed on Fridays and holidays and closes at 12.30 p.m. on the eve of a holiday.

Model of Ancient Jerusalem (Holyland Hotel): 8 a.m. to 5 p.m. in summer, 8 a.m. to 4 p.m. in winter.

Mosque of Makhpelah (Hebron): 7.30 to 11.30 a.m. and 1.30 to 3 p.m. (till 4 or 5 p.m. in summer) every day except Friday.

Museum of the Jewish Diaspora (Tel Aviv/Ramat Aviv): 1 a.m. to 5 p.m. on Sundays, Mondays and Thursdays, 3 to 10 p.m. on Tuesdays and Wednesdays.

Natural History Museum: 10 a.m. to 1 p.m. daily except Saturdays when hours are 10.30 a.m. to 1.30 p.m. (Wednesdays and Thursdays also from 4 to 6 p.m.).

Old Yishuv Court Museum: 10 a.m. to 5 p.m. daily except on Fridays and eves of holidays when hours are from 10 a.m. to 1 p.m.

Pontifical Biblical Institute: 9 a.m. to 2 p.m. except Sundays and Catholic holidays.

President's House: 8.30 to 10.30 a.m. on Sundays and Thursdays.

S   **Rockefeller Museum:** 10 a.m. to 2 p.m. Friday and Saturday, 10 a.m. to 5 p.m. other days.

Shrine of the Book (Israel Museum): same as Museum except Tuesday: 10 a.m. to 10 p.m.

Simon Peter's house and **Capernaum's synagogue** (Capernaum): 8 a.m. to 4 p.m. daily.

Sound and Light Show (Citadel): every evening, except Friday and holidays, from April to October at 7.30, Hebrew, 8.45, English; Monday, Tuesday, Wednesday and Saturday at 10 p.m. English.

Temple Mount: 8 a.m. to 4 p.m. daily.

Tombs of the Prophets: 8 a.m. to 3 p.m. daily except Saturday.

Tombs of the Sanhedrin: 9 a.m. to sunset daily except Saturday.

YMCA (lift): 9 a.m. to 3 p.m. weekdays, 9 a.m. to 1 p.m. on Saturdays.

STREET NAMES. There is something resembling confusion in street names of Jerusalem, written in Hebrew, Arabic, and as often as not, English. The Hebrew word for street is *Rehov*. King George Street, for example, can be called just King George Street, or alternatively HaMelekh George Street, Rehov King George or Rehov HaMelekh George. The only rule: the name itself is what matters, i.e. (King) George. So in this book we have kept to the English forms—which is, in fact, what you'll probably be using most.

T   **TIME DIFFERENCES.** Israel keeps the same time all year. The chart below shows the time differences between Israel and various cities in winter.

New York	London	**Jerusalem**	Johannesburg	Sydney	Auckland
5 a.m.	10 a.m.	**noon**	noon	9 p.m.	11 p.m.

TIPPING. (For specific recommendations, see inside back-cover.) Israel is very egalitarian in spirit, and tipping is not a hallowed institution among its citizens. You needn't tip taxi drivers, or waiters in cafés and restaurants who add a service charge to your bill. If not included, a few coins will suffice. If someone picks up your tip with indifference, it could be that no tip was expected rather than that the tip is too little. In establishments which cater mainly to foreign tourists, such as the larger hotels, tips are more readily received.

TOILETS. Public toilets are scattered throughout East and West Jerusalem, in the busier sections. Signs at streetcorners nearby point the way in Hebrew, Arabic and English. Toilets may be marked *W. C.* (for "water closet"), *00* or *Toilet,* with the familiar male and female silhouettes. Tipping is not necessary.

TOURIST INFORMATION OFFICES. Israel Government Tourist Offices (I.G.T.O.) in other countries, and Tourist Information Offices in Israel are ready to help with maps, brochures and all sorts of information.

Australia: Carlton Centre, 55 Elizabeth Street, Sydney, N.S.W. 2000; tel.: 233-1044. Cable: Tourisrael Sydney.

Canada: 102 Bloor Street west, Toronto 181, Ontario M5S 1M8; tel.: (416) 964-3784. Cable: Tourisrael Toronto.

South Africa: 915 Rand Central, 165 Jeppe Street, Johannesburg; tel.: 23-8931/2. Cable: Tourisrael Johannesburg.

United Kingdom: 59, St. James's Street, London SW1A 1LL; tel.: (01) 493-2431. Cable: Tourisrael London SW1.

U.S.A.: 488 Madison Avenue, New York, N.Y. 10022; tel.: (212) 754–0140. Cable: Tourisrael New York.

6380 Wilshire Boulevard, Los Angeles, CA 90048; tel.: (213) 658-7462. Cable: Tourisrael Losangeles.

5 South Wabash Avenue, Chicago, IL 60603; tel.: (312) 782-4306. Cable: Tourisrael Chicago.

795 Peachtree Street N.E., Atlanta, GA 30308; tel.: (404) 873-1470. Cable: Tourisrael Atlanta.

In Jerusalem, Government Tourist Offices are at:
24 King George Street; tel.: (02) 241281/2
and
Jaffa Gate in the Old City; tel.: (02) 282295/6.

The Jerusalem Municipal Tourist Information Office:
34 Jaffa (Yafo) Road; tel. (02) 228844.

After 6 p.m. you can dial (02) 241197 for details on what's happening in Jerusalem. A recorded message will tell you the events of the evening. **123**

T **TOURS.** See also GUIDES AND INTERPRETERS. You can learn all about Jerusalem without spending a single shekel by going on one of the many free tours organized by the Jerusalem Municipality and many other civic and religious groups. Tours are especially plentiful during religious festival periods. Check *Events in the Jerusalem Region*, a free bulletin of current events handed out in hotels and tourist information offices.

Tour companies and travel agencies offer city tours at reasonable prices, and these provide an easy and comfortable way to see the sights in outlying areas. Those with time to visit other parts of the country should consider going with a group if their destination is within the West Bank territories. Tour operators keep well up on unrest in sensitive areas, and steer clear of trouble.

TRANSPORT

Buses: When Jerusalem was reunified in 1967, it had two bus companies. It still does. East Jerusalem is served from the terminal called the Old City Bus Station, on Sultan Suleiman Street near Damascus Gate. Bus No. 22 goes to Jaffa Gate, Talpiot, Rachel's Tomb and Bethlehem; No. 23 will take you to Hebron; and No. 75 climbs to the top of the Mount of Olives.

West Jerusalem's Central Bus Station, on Jaffa Road in the Etz Haim quarter, handles traffic to the greater part of Jerusalem and to other Israeli cities and towns. Bus service is suspended in West Jerusalem and throughout Israel on the Jewish Sabbath and on Jewish holidays. Arab-operated buses in East Jerusalem run every day.

Taxis: Most taxis belong to agencies and are well controlled. Some drivers cannot resist trying their luck on tourists, however, and even on local people. Although taxis have meters and fares are fixed by the government, in practice some cabbies prefer to haggle out other arrangements, so make very sure in advance if there is the slightest doubt. The best thing is to rely on the official agencies at the Gates of the Old City, or call, in the New City, the numbers below and you will be picked up in a few minutes (always specify the number of people travelling).

222221/22/23/24; 233233; or 664444/634444.

Sheruts: These shared taxis, usually eight-seater Mercedes, circulate round Jerusalem's streets on Friday evenings and Saturdays from as soon as West Jerusalem's bus service stops running until the moment it restarts. They also pick up passengers after the last bus each day. **124** *Sheruts* will let you get off where you like, although they do have regular stops. You can hail one just as you can a taxi. Ask, however, before you even step in if it is, in fact, a *sherut* and not a regular taxi.

Sheruts also offer the fastest and most comfortable means of inter-city travel, at fares only slightly higher than those of the bus. Except for the special Jerusalem–Ben Gurion airport run, it is not necessary to reserve seats for inter-city travel. Most *sherut* booking agencies are near Zion Square in Jaffa Road. Inter-city tariffs are fixed by the government and are higher on Sabbaths and holidays and after the last buses.

Trains: Few people travel by train to and from Jerusalem any more, as bus and *sherut* service is so quick and inexpensive. A few trains leave daily for Tel Aviv, Haifa and Beersheba, and points along the way. For information, dial 71 77 64.

WATER. Tap water is drinkable in Jerusalem and throughout Israel, though it is not always very tasty. Your hotel may provide you with a carafe of water, and in Arab hotels the carafe may be an earthen jug set in a basin—water evaporates slowly from the porous jug and keeps it delightfully cool. In larger hotels and restaurants, and in many pharmacies, European mineral waters are on sale.

SOME USEFUL EXPRESSIONS

	Hebrew	Arabic
yes/no	**ken/lo**	*náam/la*
please/thank you	**bevakashá/todá**	*lútfan/shókran*
excuse me	**slikhá**	*ádam muákhaze*
Do you speak English?	**atá medabér anglít**	*btitkállem inglízi*
What does this mean?	**ma hainýan**	*shu máanah háda*
Waiter (Waitress), please.	**meltzár (meltzarít)**	*ísmaya*
I'd like…	**aní rotzé**	*bíddi*
How much is that?	**káma ze olé**	*háda bikám*
What time is it?	**ma hashaá**	*eh elwákt*
Could you tell me…?	**tukhál lomár li**	*ull li*
Where are the toilets?	**eyfó hasherutím**	*fen elmaráhid*
Help me, please.	**azór li, bevakashá**	*sáedni*

Index

An asterisk (*) next to a page number indicates a map reference. For index to Practical Information, see p. 105.

4/82 RP